ROOTED

DEEPENING YOUR RELATIONSHIP WITH JESUS

BRAD WHITT
FOREWORD BY KEN WHITTEN

innovopublishing.com

Published by Innovo Publishing, LLC
www.innovopublishing.com
1-888-546-2111

Publishing quality books, eBooks, audiobooks, music, screenplays & courses for the Christian & wholesome markets since 2008.

ROOTED
Deepening Your Relationship with Jesus

Copyright © 2023 by Brad Whitt
All rights reserved.

No part of this publication may be reproduced, stored in a retrieval system, or transmitted in any form or by any means electronic, mechanical, photocopying, recording, or otherwise, without the prior written permission of the Author.

Unless otherwise noted, all scripture is taken from the New King James Version®. Copyright © 1982 by Thomas Nelson. Used by permission. All rights reserved.

ISBN: 978-1-61314-920-1

Cover Design & Interior Layout: Innovo Publishing, LLC

Printed in the United States of America
U.S. Printing History
First Edition: 2015
Second Edition: 2023

Has God called you to create a Christ-centered or wholesome book, eBook, audiobook, music album, screenplay, or online course? Visit Innovo's educational center (cpportal.com) to learn how to accomplish your calling with excellence.

CONTENTS

Foreword
vii

1. **SAVED, SAVED, SAVED**
~ *9* ~

2. **BEGINNING RIGHT**
~ *23* ~

3. **SPIRITUAL WARFARE**
~ *37* ~

4. **ROOTED IN THE WORD**
~ *51* ~

5. **ROOTED IN PRAYER**
~ *71* ~

6. **SHARE JESUS WITHOUT FEAR**
~ *83* ~

7. **GROWING IN GIVING**
~ *97* ~

8. **FIRST PLACE**
~ *109* ~

Endnotes
117

FOREWORD

When I was a little boy growing up in Illinois, right outside my bedroom window were two giant weeping willow trees providing shade and beauty for the entire neighborhood. These trees native to China are graceful deciduous trees that grow 45 to 70 feet with a crown of flowing branches that can be just as wide. Interesting thing about willow trees: their roots grow more rapidly after they are pruned.

You know, Jesus thought the same thing. He said in John 15:1-3, "I am the true vine, and My Father is the vinedresser. Every branch in me that does not bear fruit, He takes away; and every branch that bears fruit He prunes, that it may bear more fruit."

In Psalm 1, the Hebrew songwriter says the blessed man is the person "who is like a tree planted by the rivers of water who brings forth his fruit in its season, and whatsoever he does, shall prosper."

The oak tree roots are relatively shallow but make up for it in their lateral spread. The roots of a mature oak tree can spread outward 75–250 feet. An oak tap root grows to a depth of 3–5 feet. The lateral roots can grow 3–7 times the circumference of the oak's branches. What we know about oak tree roots is they spread outward, more than downward. According to Jim Urban, a noted tree and soil expert "Trees are genetically capable of growing deep roots but root architecture is strongly influenced by two things: soil and climate conditions."

What you are holding in your hands is a very practical guide to the soil and climate conditions of your spiritual life.

Author and teacher Brad Whitt, in his book *Rooted*, helps us to understand it's OK to be deep, but if you want real influence and you desire your spiritual life to reach outward to others, the conditions of both soil and climate must be met to the fullest. Of course the soil is your heart, and the climate is the habits of your life.

As you walk through this helpful, practical book, you're going to discover on this journey that growth begins with finding Jesus as Lord and King of your life and ends with seeking Jesus and His kingdom. The roots grow deeper and wider as we obey, first in baptism and then in the disciplines of immersing ourselves into God's Word, prayer, sharing our faith, and growing in the stewardship of our giving.

FOREWORD

Lastly, those roots are there to stay when we come to understand God has called us not to worry but to "seek first the Kingdom of God." In other words, Jesus tells us in Matthew 6, "Don't worry about food, finances, fitness, or even your future." He's got us covered. In fact, Jesus is saying, "If you want to change your emotion, you have to shift your devotion." When our motion and devotion is all about Jesus and being rooted in Him, we will be a force to be reckoned with as we engage in spiritual warfare. And always remember this: We win!

No wonder Paul reminded the church in Colossae, "As you have received Christ Jesus the Lord, so walk in Him, rooted and built up in him and established in the faith, as you have been taught abounding in it with thanksgiving" (Col. 2:6-7).

C'mon, let's take this journey together. Let's grow together in the knowledge and grace of our Lord Jesus Christ and let our roots run deep and wide, for the gospel of Jesus Christ and His kingdom. You're going to love this book—simple yet profound. May the conditions of our heart and habits be forever changed because we are Rooted in Him.

—*Ken Whitten, National Director of Pastoral Leadership, NAMB*

1

SAVED, SAVED, SAVED

(Colossians 2:6–7)

Our family recently took a vacation. On the way, we passed some palm trees that were propped up by 2 X 4s.

I had these trees on my mind when we arrived at our destination in Charleston, S.C. We took a tour of the Legare Waring House in Charleston and enjoyed the beauty of the Avenue of Oaks. I couldn't help but contrast these magnificent oaks that covered the walkway with the palm trees that had to be propped up externally to be supported. What was the difference?

Roots.

The oaks are rooted. "The root system of a mature oak tree can total hundreds of miles. They may…occupy a space four to seven times the width of the tree's crown."[1] In contrast, the root system of a palm tree is quite small. Paul says we are to be like those oaks:

> *As you therefore have received Christ Jesus the Lord, so walk in Him, rooted and built up in Him and established in the faith, as you have been taught, abounding in it with thanksgiving. (Colossians 2:6–7)*

This book is about how you can be rooted deeply in Christ. Here are some of the benefits you can look forward to as you become rooted in Christ:

- *Stability.* People who are deeply rooted will withstand the storms of life. They are like the wise man that built his house on a rock. They are not shaken by the storms of life. They are not "tossed to and fro and carried about with every wind of doctrine, by the trickery of men, in the cunning craftiness of deceitful plotting" (Ephesians 4:14).
- *Continual nourishment.* Rooted people have a deep source of spiritual nourishment which continually feeds them. They are like a tree, planted by the streams of water which bears its fruit in season (Psalm 1).
- *Joy.* Jesus said, "If you keep My commandments, you will abide in My love, just as I have kept My Father's commandments and abide in His love. These things I have spoken to you, that My joy may remain in you, and that your joy may be full"(John 15:10-11). The happiest people on the planet are people who are rooted in Christ.
- *Fruitfulness.* Rooted plants are fruit-bearing plants. "I am the vine, you are the branches. He who abides in Me, and I in him, bears much fruit; for without Me you can do nothing" (John 15:5). Jesus didn't say we would be even more fruitful if we abide in Christ. He said that without Christ we can do nothing. Rooted in Christ, we will bear much fruit. It is an all or nothing deal.
- *Peace.* There is peace in knowing that your roots go down deep. There is peace in knowing you can withstand every drought and storm. "Peace I leave with you, My peace I give to you; not as the world gives do I give to you. Let not your heart be troubled, neither let it be afraid" (John 14:27). The Bible describes it as a peace that surpasses all understanding (Philippians 4.6-7).
- *Assurance of our salvation.* God's will for every believer is that you have absolute confidence in your salvation. God wants you to know that you will go to Heaven when you die. Rooted people know. They don't just hope; they know.

- *Spiritual growth.* You can't grow up unless your roots go down. Only rooted people grow. "That Christ may dwell in your hearts through faith; that you, being rooted and grounded in love, may be able to comprehend with all the saints what is the width and length and depth and height—to know the love of Christ which passes knowledge; that you may be filled with all the fullness of God" (Ephesians 3:17-19).
- *Purpose.* When our roots go down deep, we discover why God put us here. We discover that "We are God's workmanship, created in Christ Jesus for good works, which God prepared beforehand that we should walk in them" (Ephesians 2:10). We discover what good works God has prepared in advance for us to do. There is nothing like living life on purpose. Only rooted people know this joy.

Being rooted has many benefits: stability, continual nourishment, joy, fruitfulness, peace, assurance of salvation, and purpose. How do we become rooted?

ROOTED STARTS WITH BEING PLANTED

Many don't get rooted because they were never planted. Jesus taught that many will be surprised on the judgment day:

> *"Many will say to Me in that day, 'Lord, Lord, have we not prophesied in Your name, cast out demons in Your name, and done many wonders in Your name?' And then I will declare to them, 'I never knew you; depart from Me, you who practice lawlessness!'" (Matthew 7:22-23)*

I think if Jesus were writing today, He might say, "Many will say to me on that day, 'Didn't I walk down the aisle and sign the card and get baptized and attend church and give and serve and live a decent life?' And then I will declare, 'Depart from me; I never knew you.'"

There are two lessons from this teaching. One is that many will be surprised on judgment day. The second is that assurance of eternal life is based on a relationship with Jesus. Jesus did not say...

- Depart from Me, you were not a church member.
- Depart from Me, you did not give.

- Depart from Me, you were not good enough.
- Depart from Me, you were not baptized.

Jesus said, "Depart from Me, I never knew you." Christianity is all about knowing Jesus. It is all about relationship. Jesus knows every true child of God.

The question is: Do you know Him?

Billy Graham has often been credited with the declaration that the greatest mission field in the world is the members of American churches.[2] Many are lost! They have never tapped into the tree of life. They have never been grafted in by the grace of God. They are still in the sinful soil of this wicked world. They cannot grow because they have never been planted in God's vineyard.

Going to church doesn't make you a Christian any more than sitting in a garden makes you a gardenia.

Many others are saved, but they have not grown. They are planted, but they have not produced much fruit. They don't know how to stand on the principles of God. They do not know how to walk in the power of the Spirit of God. They do not know how to lean on the promises of God. Their roots do not go down deep. They view salvation as the end.

Salvation is, in a way, the end. It is the front end.

Many never lay hold of the victorious, joyful, John 10:10, abundant Christian life.

Like those pitiful, propped up palm trees, they have to be propped up because their roots don't go down deep. They want to be entertained more than they want to be fed. They want to be dazzled more than they want to be discipled. They want to be cheered more than they want to be challenged.

Entertainment may build a crowd, but it does not build disciples. Churches can get a crowd with feel-good preaching, but they can only make disciples by proclaiming the message of Jesus:

> *Then He said to them all, "If anyone desires to come after Me, let him deny himself, and take up his cross daily, and follow Me. For whoever desires to save his life will lose it, but whoever loses his life for My sake will save it. For what profit is it to a man if he gains the whole world, and is himself destroyed or lost? For whoever is ashamed of Me and My words, of him the*

Son of Man will be ashamed when He comes in His own glory, and in His Father's, and of the holy angels. (Luke 9:23–26)

The greatest miracle of God is that He can change sinners. God can take greedy people and turn them into generous people. God can take worried people and give them the peace that surpasses all understanding. God can take mean people and turn them into kind people. How does that happen?

Growth starts with being born. Spiritual growth starts with being born again.

THE MEANING OF SALVATION

The word "salvation" has lost its pizzazz for some of us. We have heard it so many times that we find ourselves looking at our watches when we hear the word.

"Salvation" basically means to deliver or rescue. It means to get out of trouble. It was often used in a non-theological sense in the New Testament. For example, Peter used the word when he was walking on the water and looked at the waves and a man-hole opened up beneath him, "Lord, save me" (Matthew 14:30). Peter didn't have theology or eternal destiny in mind. He needed help… now!

The word is translated "deliverance" in Philippians 1:19, but it is the same underlying Greek word that is normally translated "salvation." "For I know that this will turn out for my deliverance" (Philippians 1:19).

Similarly, it is translated "survival" in this verse: "Therefore I urge you to take nourishment, for this is for your survival, since not a hair will fall from the head of any of you" (Acts 27:34).

Like many theological words, it was an ordinary word used in ordinary life before it was a theological word. One Greek dictionary explains, "These terms first refer to salvation (human or divine) from serious peril. Curing from illness is another sense. Horses may save in battle, or night may save an army from destruction, good counsel may save ships, etc."[3]

This helps us to understand why some don't get that excited about the concept of salvation; some don't see themselves as in trouble. Only people who realize they are in danger of drowning are excited about the Lifeguard.

"Saved" always has to do with the idea of "saved from something." If we don't see ourselves as in trouble, then getting saved doesn't mean that much to us.

This is why there are two thousand years of Old Testament history that preceded the coming of Christ. It was to create a people who understood the idea that God is holy and we are sinners.

The temple architecture was one example of this. It was set up with various spaces, and you had to get cleaned up to enter. The center of the temple was the Holy of Holies. This was only entered by a priest, and that only happened one time a year. They would put some bells on his robe so in case he died they could know because the bell would quit jingling. They tied a rope around his leg so they could pull him out in such a case. This was one of many ways the message was reinforced: God is holy. We are sinners. You can't rush into God's presence.

Every year at the temple small animals had their throats cut to remind people that we are sinners and, when someone sins, someone has to pay. Imagine growing up where every year you went to the temple and watched a priest slit the throat of one of your pets. You cry and ask your parents, "Why? Why? Why?"

Your parents lovingly respond, "Because we are sinners. God is holy. You are a sinner. I am a sinner. Sin must be paid for. We must be saved from our sin." This happened year after year, generation after generation. The result was a people who understood that we have a problem. We need to be saved.

The movie Apollo 13 made famous the line, "Houston, we have a problem." In America today, many of us don't feel we have a problem. This is the challenge of communicating the gospel. We must communicate two truths:

- *God is holy.* He cannot stand to look at sin. We are, in the words of Jonathan Edwards, "Sinners in the hands of an angry God." The Bible says, "For all have sinned and fall short of the glory of God" (Romans 3:23). Even our goodness is tainted with selfish, unclean motives: "But we are all like an unclean thing, And all our righteousnesses are like filthy rags" (Isaiah 64:6). We are sinners by nature and sinners by choice.

  There is a reason God can't stand to look a sin. Sin is the stuff that messes up our lives. Sin always harms. It always makes life worse in the long run.

Dr. Tony Evans states it so well. "One reason we don't have a high view of sin today is because we have a low view of God."[4]

- *God is crazy about us.* He watched his own Son die so that we could have a relationship.

MY FAVORITE ILLUSTRATION OF SALVATION

The best illustration of what it means to be saved that I have ever heard is told by Paul Harvey. He tells the story of a Boston preacher named S.D. Gordon.[5]

> "S.D. Gordon waited until the service had started before he burst through the back doors with an old, rusty, wire bird cage. He set it on the pulpit to incite curiosity. As people sang, they could see the wire bird cage, and it did what Gordon wanted it to do: it made them good and curious.
>
> "Yesterday, I met a boy with this bird cage. In that bird cage were three common sparrows. I asked the boy what he was going to do with those birds. The boy described all kinds of cruelty he had planned for those birds. He said he was going to pull their feathers. He said he was going to try to get them to fight each other. He said he was going to starve them. He said he was going to abuse them and finally let his cats eat them.
>
> "I asked the boy what he wanted for those birds. The boy told me the birds were not worth anything. He told me they couldn't sing. They were not pretty. They were beat up from his abuse. I asked him what he wanted for them. I paid him his price—$10.
>
> "I took this wire bird cage to the edge of town, opened the door, and set the birds free.
>
> "One day Satan was coming out of the Garden of Eden. He was gloating and boasting, and he had a cage. He said he had set a trap and had caught all of humanity in that trap. He said he was going to abuse them and torture them and get them to fight. Then, he was going to kill them.

"Jesus said, 'How much will you take for those people?'

"Satan said, 'You don't want them. They would be of no value to you. They'll sneer at you and reject you and won't love or follow you. They will spit on you and curse you. You don't want them.'

"'How much do you want?'

"'The price is too high. I want all of your blood.'

"Jesus paid it all."

I love the song:[6]

He paid a debt He did not owe;
I owed a debt I could not pay;
I needed someone to wash my sins away.
And, now, I sing a brand new song,
"Amazing Grace."
Christ Jesus paid a debt that I could never pay.

John Stott said that the essence of sin is man substituting himself for God; the essence of salvation is God substituting Himself for man.[7]

SAVED TO SIN NO MORE

God not only saves us from the penalty of sin; He also saves us from the power of sin.

Once we are saved, we no longer have to sin. As the old hymn writer put it, we are "slaves to sin no more."

Before you are saved, you don't have a choice; you are a slave to sin. But, once you are saved, you no longer have to sin. Not that we will ever lay hold of this perfectly and become sinless, but the fact remains we no longer have to sin.

If we are truly saved, we will sin less than we did before. If we don't sin less than we did before, it calls into question whether we were truly saved. We are saved by grace through faith alone. But faith that saves is never alone.

Buddy Robinson was a tongue-tied preacher who used to say, "Before I was saved, I used to drink and cuss and run around with wild women. Since I have been saved and sanctified, I have just about cut out all that."

We will never be completely sinless. The day we are sinless is the day the mortician is getting our name right for the newspaper.

You can sin. You can sin and enjoy it. But you cannot sin and enjoy it for long. The heavenly Father disciplines those He loves (Hebrews 12).

Eventually, we will be saved from the presence of sin. 1 John 3:2 says that when we see Him, we will be like Him.

One of these days the trumpet will sound and the sky will split open. He will take us away from this world of wickedness and sorrow and tears and shame.

The first time He came to redeem me.
The second time He will come to receive me.
The first time He came to give me a new heart.
The second time He will come to give me a new home.
The first time He came to give me His grace.
The second time He will come to give me His glory.

F.F. Bruce once said, "Sanctification is glory begun. Glorification is sanctification complete."[8]

I have been saved. I am being saved. One day, I will be saved.

THE METHOD OF SALVATION

Salvation begins and ends with God. It was God's idea. It was God's purpose. It was God's design.

It is God that does the convicting. It is God that does the drawing. It is God that convinces us of sin. We must respond by repentance and faith, but it is still true what Jonah said, "Salvation is of the Lord" (Jonah 2:9).

Salvation was in the heart of God before the world was created. God had the solution before sin came into the world.

Has it ever occurred to you that nothing ever occurs to God? God has never said, "Oops." God has never learned anything. God doesn't have or need a backup plan. God never has to have a mulligan. The Bible says, "He chose us in Him before the foundation of the world" (Ephesians 1:4). John said, "We love Him because He first loved us" (1 John 4:19).

In using the word "chose" (Ephesians 1:4), Paul introduces his greatest treatment of what is known as "the doctrine of election." This doctrine has been greatly misunderstood by many. Some have placed all of the emphasis of salvation on God's sovereignty. They view salvation as God choosing certain individuals to the exclusion of everybody else. Others view salvation as something a person can choose whenever or however they wish. Both of these views are wrong.

Dr. Hershel Hobbs puts it this way. "Basically, election means that God has taken the initiative in His purpose to save men. Apart from that initiative no man can be saved. Therefore, election should not be viewed as God's purpose to save as few but as many as possible. To relate election to the few is to ignore the many exhortations to preach the gospel to all men. And it runs head-on into such phrases as 'whosever believeth' (John 3:16) and 'whosoever will' or is willing (Revelation 22:17; see Isaiah 55:1).[9]

Years ago, John MacArthur was preaching at Adrian Roger's church. John MacArthur is a Calvinist and preached a strong sermon on predestination. In his typical, gracious way, Adrian Rogers closed the service with these words, "Isn't it amazing how many get elected in a red-hot revival service?"

Salvation was thought by the Father and bought by the Son.

HOW DO YOU SPELL SALVATION?

Many want to spell salvation "d-o." They say you have to do something to be saved. They say you have to attend this and go there and walk an aisle. Some say you have to fill out a card or pray a prayer or join a church. Some say you have to be baptized or clean up your act in certain ways.

Many want to spell salvation "d-o-n-'t." For this crowd, it is not so much about what you do as what you refrain from doing. Don't murder. Don't lie. Don't rob. Don't gossip. Don't commit adultery. According to this crowd, if you don't do bad things, you will get to go to Heaven when you die.

Salvation is not spelled "d-o."

Salvation is not spelled "d-o-n-'t."

Salvation is spelled "d-o-n-e." This is why Jesus declared on the cross, "It is finished" (John 19:30). This phrase is one word in Greek (telestai) and means "paid in full." When you make that last payment you can say, "It is finished." It is done. We have bills from the ancient world that stamped with the word telestai—paid in full.

Salvation was thought by the Father and bought by the Son. It is wrought by the working of the Holy Spirit in our lives. Jesus said,

"And when He has come, He will convict the world of sin, and of righteousness, and of judgment" (John 16:8).

J. Vernon McGee tells the story of a child that came forward during the invitation. The counselor who greeted him asked him why he was there. He explained that he got saved and wanted to tell the world. The counselor asked how he got saved.

"I did my part, and God did His part" was the boy's explanation.

"What was your part and what was God's part?"

"My part was sinning. God's part was saving."

That is how it was for me. I did the running; He did the searching. I did the sinning; He did the saving. I did the falling; He picked me up.

GOD PROTECTS THOSE HE PARENTS

We are God's children and are protected by Him. God's great salvation doesn't just keep us from sin and Hell. His salvation keeps us for all eternity.

If you are saved, Heaven is a sure thing. The Bible says, "These things I have written to you who believe in the name of the Son of God, that you may know that you have eternal life, and that you may continue to believe in the name of the Son of God" (1 John 5:13).

God wants every believer to live with the steadfast confidence that their sins are forgiven and they will go to Heaven when they die. It is not "Hope so; maybe so; think so." It is "Know so."

The Bible says we are "kept by the power of God" (1 Peter 1:5). The word kept means guarded. It was commonly used as a military term. It means that God is keeping watch over and protecting.

Recently we had something wake us up in the middle of the night. My wife awoke me with, "Did you hear that?"

Now, at my house, we are protected by Colt and insured by Smith and Wesson. I saw a sign that I want to get for my house; it read, "We don't dial 9-1-1."

I put a bullet in the chamber and handed the gun to my wife. I said, "Go check it out. See who is down there. Deal with it."

Do you think I really did that?

You know I didn't because you know that a good groom always protects his bride, and a good father always protects his children. God is the groom who protects. God is the Father and always protects.

Many believers seem to think it is our job to protect our salvation. It is not. It is God's job. It is God who protects. He protects us from the world without. He protects us from the flesh within. We are protected from the devil around. He protects our mind. He protects our heart. He protects our spirit, soul, and body.

The same Power that created the sun and the moon and the stars is protecting us. The same Power that caused Jesus to be born of a virgin, live a sinless life, die on the cross, and be raised from the dead is within us protecting us.

His protection is forever. It is eternal.

I'll close this chapter with this story. A fireman was called to a fire at a four-story apartment complex. They were able to evacuate everyone except one boy and his parents. The only window to this boy's fourth-story apartment was on the back side of the building, and there was no way they could get a ladder up to it.

The fireman noticed there was a cast-iron pipe that ran all the way up the side of the building right next to the window of the boy's apartment. The fireman shimmied up that pipe. The heat was so intense that it burned through his protective gloves. Still, he was able to save the boy.

The boy was saved. (Note, by the way, how we continue to use that word in a non-theological context.) The boy was saved, but he was now an orphan. His parents didn't make it out of the fire.

Some time passed, and there was a hearing to decide who could adopt this young boy. Because of the publicity of the event, there were a number of qualified candidates.

The first person who wanted to adopt the boy was a doctor. In fact, it was the doctor who cared for him after he was taken from the fire and brought to the Emergency Room. He said his heart was drawn to the boy from that experience.

A wealthy businessman stepped forward and asked to be considered. He said he could provide all of the boy's financial needs and most of his wants.

A college professor stepped forward and talked about the value of education. He argued he would be able to give this boy whatever tutoring he might need. He promised that if they would let him adopt the boy, he would make sure the boy got a world-class education.

The final candidate stepped forward. He was a working-class man. He wasn't wealthy. He wasn't educated. He admitted as much to the court. The judge asked him why he should be considered to adopt the boy. The man held up his blistered hands that had been burned in rescuing the child. "I ask you to allow me to adopt the boy based on these." He held up his hands. "These are the hands that saved him."

Jesus stands before all humanity with scarred hands and says, "I want to save you."

Remember the birdcage story? You are the bird in the rusty old birdcage, and Jesus says He wants to set you free.

It is pretty simple, really. The Bible says, "Whoever calls on the name of the LORD shall be saved" (Romans 10:13). Call out to Jesus. Admit you are a sinner. Tell Him you want to turn from your sin. Tell Him you want Him to run your life. He will not turn you away. It is the first step in being rooted.

You can summarize what it means to be saved this way: it is accepting the fact that God accepts you. It is accepting the fact that God is good and is a rewarder of those who seek Him (Hebrews 11:6). It is admitting that we are sinners and that sinning has not worked out so well for us. We want to be helped. We want to be saved.

Really, if you want to be saved, it comes down to this: just ask.

2

BEGINNING RIGHT

Acts 8

When I was growing up, I worked for my grandfather, who was a contractor. He reduced some important wisdom into pithy statements:

- Measure twice; cut once.
- An honest day's work for an honest day's pay.
- Make sure your thumb is out of the way before you hit the nail with the hammer. (This may not roll off the tongue like the others, but if you keep this in mind, it will keep other words from rolling off your tongue!)
- If you want it to be square when it's done, it's got to be square when it's begun.

There is a lot of wisdom packed in that last statement. If you want to end right, you have got to start right. That is true in construction, that is true in business, that is true in marriage, and it is true in Christian living. If you want to enjoy the John 10:10 abundant Christian life, you have to make sure you start right. Many Christians are saved, but they have never made much progress in their Christian life because they have not gotten started right.

It is clear how we ought to begin: baptism. Jesus taught it was the first step: "'Go therefore and make disciples of all the nations, baptizing them in the name of the Father and of the Son and of the Holy Spirit, teaching them to observe all things that I have commanded you; and lo, I am with you always, even to the end of the age.' Amen" (Matthew 28:19–20).

Jesus taught baptism was the first step in making a disciple. The early church followed His teaching. Baptism was routinely practiced by the early church immediately after salvation. Here are a few examples:

- "Then those who gladly received his word were baptized; and that day about three thousand souls were added to them" (Acts 2:41).
- "But when they believed Philip as he proclaimed the good news of the kingdom of God and the name of Jesus Christ, they were baptized, both men and women" (Acts 8:12 NIV).
- "Now a certain woman named Lydia heard us. She was a seller of purple from the city of Thyatira, who worshiped God. The Lord opened her heart to heed the things spoken by Paul. And when she and her household were baptized…" (Acts 16:14-15).

Paul's letters indicate that baptism was clearly important to the practice of the early church. A few examples:

- "Or do you not know that as many of us as were baptized into Christ Jesus were baptized into His death? Therefore we were buried with Him through baptism into death, that just as Christ was raised from the dead by the glory of the Father, even so we also should walk in newness of life" (Romans 6:3–4).
- "For by one Spirit we were all baptized into one body—whether Jews or Greeks, whether slaves or free—and have all been made to drink into one Spirit" (1 Corinthians 12:13)
- "For as many of you as were baptized into Christ have put on Christ" (Galatians 3:27)

Yet, with all this emphasis on baptism in the New Testament, it doesn't seem all that important to many believers today. I have done enough sermons on baptism to tell you without hesitation that when I bring the subject up, people tend to look at their watches. Sermons on baptism don't get the most downloads on our website.

Why does baptism seem to be so important to God and does not seem to be important to the rest of us? What does it do for the believer? What are we missing?

For some, the topic of baptism seems boring and irrelevant. It doesn't seem that important. It sounds like a religious ritual—an antiquated practice of a by-gone era. The Bible does not present it that way.

It is a normal part of Christian living in the New Testament.

For many, the teaching on baptism is a very controversial subject. It is a subject over which much ink has been spilt in the theological literature. Denominations agree on many issues but will disagree on baptism. Yet, the Bible's teaching on the subject is clear-cut and easy to understand.

For others, baptism is a very sensitive subject. It is very emotional. I have talked to many about baptism over the years, and before long, the conversation got very heated. When you begin asking what baptism is and is not, you touch a nerve.

In this chapter, we want to take a straightforward look at what the Bible teaches about baptism.

Baptism is important. It was important to Jesus, and it was important to the early church. Yet, for many modern churches, the subject is practically ignored. Adrian Rogers used to say, "We must never minimize what the Bible has so clearly emphasized."

Where there is no emphasis on baptism, there will be no experience of baptism. Perhaps this de-emphasis on baptism explains why my denomination is seeing the lowest rates of baptism in sixty years.

I heard of one preacher who emphasized baptism so much he preached on it every Sunday. Finally, his deacons confronted him about the practice and suggested they assign him his preaching topics.

Looking for a topic that would not lead to baptism, they assigned the preacher the topic of preaching on pills. (Stay with me here.)

His sermon went something like this: Today, I am assigned by the deacons the topic of preaching on pills. Now, there are big pills and small pills, bitter pills and sweet pills. There are expensive pills and cheap pills and pills of every imaginable color. The most important pill is the gos-pill. And, when you respond to the gospel, the next step is to be baptized.

Why was baptism so important to this preacher? Why was it so important to the Christ and the early church? Why should it be important to us?

BAPTISM MEANS YOU ARE INCLUDED IN THE BODY OF CHRIST

Baptism means you are one of us. Baptism means you are part of the group. Baptism means you belong.

From the time we are small children, we all have a strong urge to belong. C.S. Lewis wrote an excellent article on this called "The Inner Ring." In this article, Lewis described the incredible lengths people will go to be a part of the inner ring. People dress a certain way and talk a certain way and go places because they want to be in the inner ring.

Christianity offers a relationship with God, and it also offers inclusion in God's community. The rite of initiation is believer's baptism.

Groups routinely have initiation rites. To become a U.S. Citizen, you can't just sign up; you have to go through certain proscribed steps to become a citizen. Some groups have initiation rites that are quite severe:[10]

- The tribes living along the Sepik River in Papua New Guinea have used the tradition of scarification to mature their boys into men for decades. The ceremony requires the youth to be cut along his back, chest, and buttocks in elaborate patterns to mimic the coarse skin of a crocodile.
- In the South Pacific Ocean, on Pentecost Island, tribe members construct a tower sixty to ninety feet high made from the trees surrounding a clearing. Rocks and wood are removed from the ground, and the soil is tilled before the tower is built. The rickety structure is then used as the world's most extreme form of bungee jumping, with only two vines and faith supporting a diver. The ritual is done to ensure the yam harvest that year will be successful; the higher they dive, the better the harvest will be. It's also thought to strengthen participants spiritually as they take the leap of faith. While it's not required to dive, those who do are revered in the community and seen as true warriors. After all, to dive means to sacrifice your life for the tribe. They embrace the possibility of death during the

initiation; it'll be like taking one for the team. Boys around seven and eight (once they are circumcised) can participate, and they're considered men after they survive the fall.

- Papua New Guinea isn't known just for the crocodile scarification ritual mentioned earlier in the list. Deep in the highlands, an equally gruesome rite of passage exists. The Matausa believe that if a boy doesn't complete the blood initiation, he may suffer the consequences his entire life. He will never be seen as a real man, and he won't experience the vigor and strength that the others have. That's why boys are eager to go through the initiation, regardless of pain, to become warriors. In order to do this, they must cleanse themselves of any remaining female influences left in them from their mothers. First, they must slide two thin wooden canes down their throats to induce vomiting several times to empty their stomachs. Afterward, a collection of reeds is inserted into the initiate's nose to further expel bad influence. Finally, they must endure repeated stabbings to the tongue. This bloody ritual thus purifies them, and they are truly men afterward.

Baptism, by comparison, is a pretty easy rite of initiation.

Baptism is always done by a church, not an individual. It is an ordinance of the church, not a practice of an individual. John Hammond said, "There is widespread agreement that the administration of the ordinances [baptism and the Lord's Supper] belongs to the local church. This agreement is based on a number of factors. First, the command to baptize was given to the apostles, not as independent individuals, but as authorized leaders of the early church. The New Testament descriptions of baptism and the Lord's Supper seem to assume that these activities normally take place in the context of a church, or, in the case of some baptisms, at the beginning stages of a church's establishment."

Millard Erickson said, "It is almost universally agreed that baptism is in some way connected with the beginning of the Christian life; it is one's initiation into the universal, invisible church as well as the local, visible church."[11]

Matthew 16 suggests that Jesus has given all authority to the church, and it is vital to the authenticity of baptism to oversee and approve both who is baptized and who does the baptizing.

Perhaps you remember the scene with Robert Duvall in the movie *The Apostle*? Robert Duvall baptizes himself in a lake saying that, from that moment on, he is going to be God's man. A few years ago a seminary student did just this—he baptized himself. This is not biblical. Baptism is an initiation rite into the local church. It means you are part of the body. Rick Warren explains:[12]

> *In the Greek text of the Great Commission there are three participle verbs: going, baptizing, and teaching. Each of these is a part of the command to "make disciples." Going, baptizing, and teaching are the essential elements of the disciplemaking process. At first glance you might wonder why the Great Commission gives the same prominence to the simple act of baptism as it does to the great tasks of evangelism and edification. Obviously, Jesus did not mention it by accident. Why is baptism so important to warrant inclusion in Christ's Great Commission? I believe it is because it symbolizes one of the purposes of the church: fellowship—identification with the body of Christ. As Christians we're called to belong, not just to believe.*

THE NECESSITY OF COMMUNITY

Baptism is important because community is important. Baptism is always baptism into the body of Christ. The Bible teaches that we need each other. There are no Lone Ranger Christians. Even the Lone Ranger had Tonto. We really do need each other.

We need community because we were created in the image of our triune God. "The eternal triune God reveals Himself to us as Father, Son, and Holy Spirit, with distinct personal attributes, but without division of nature, essence, or being."[13] There is community in the Godhead, and we were created in His image. God Himself is the original small group.

The Bible teaches what modern science is just now discovering—life is better when lived together. Here are a few highlights:

- Dennis Proffitt at the University of Virginia found that students estimated the steepness of the grade of a hill to be much steeper if they were walking alone. The presence of a friend made it seem easier.[14] It is true what we often say at weddings: where joy is shared, it is doubled; where sorrow is shared, it is cut in half. Life is better in community.

- In a one-of-a-kind study, students at Pennsylvania State University were assigned to two groups. The first group was instructed to give or receive a minimum of five hugs per day over the course of four weeks and to record the details. The hugs had to be front-to-front (nonsexual) hugs, using both arms of both participants; however, the length and strength of the hug, as well as the placement of hands, were left to their discretion. Furthermore, these students couldn't simply hug their boyfriends or girlfriends half a dozen times; they had to aim to hug as many different individuals as possible. The second group, the controls, was instructed simply to record the number of hours they read each day over the same four weeks. The hugging group (which partook in an average of forty-nine hugs over the course of the study) became much happier.[15]

- One study was based in Alameda County, California. For nine years researchers followed 7,000 people to discern their lifestyle habits—how often they attend groups, when they go to meetings, any clubs they participate in, and so forth. In addition, they studied health rates, incidence of death, and the like. Here is what they discovered: People who are not in a group are twice as likely to die in the next year as those who are in a group.[16]

- Turns out, there was one—and only one—characteristic that distinguished the happiest ten percent from everybody else: the strength of their social relationships.[17]

Science is just now discovering what the Bible has long taught: living in community is good for you. Baptism is the initiation rite, or first step of obedience, into the community of the church.

GROWTH COMES IN COMMUNITY

Spiritual growth only happens as we are in community. You can't grow in Christ on your own. The classic verse on this is "not forsaking the assembling of ourselves together, as is the manner of some, but exhorting one another, and so much the more as you see the Day approaching" (Hebrews 10:25).

Notice this is not talking about a meeting where we sit in straight rows and watch the same events happen on the same stage. This is encouraging one another. This is circles, not rows. This is me encouraging you, and you encouraging me.

The Bible teaches we only grow as we are in relationship:

- "In whom the whole building, being fitted together, grows into a holy temple in the Lord, in whom you also are being built together for a dwelling place of God in the Spirit" (Ephesians 2:21–22).
- "But, speaking the truth in love, may grow up in all things into Him who is the head—Christ—from whom the whole body, joined and knit together by what every joint supplies, according to the effective working by which every part does its share, causes growth of the body for the edifying of itself in love" (Ephesians 4:15–16).
- "And not holding fast to the Head, from whom all the body, nourished and knit together by joints and ligaments, grows with the increase that is from God" (Colossians 2:19).
- We only grow in community. Baptism is the door to community.

THE "WHO" OF BAPTISM

I'd like to address two questions in this section:

- Who is authorized to baptize?
- Who is to be baptized?

The first question has been partially answered. Since baptism means you are included into the church, it follows that the church can authorize anyone to baptize. The converse is this: no one is authorized to baptize except that a church has authorized them to do so. A lone individual baptizing independent of a local church is not biblical.

The answer to the second question is equally straightforward. In the Bible, only believers are baptized. This necessarily excludes infants from baptism. There are no examples or hints of infant baptism in the

Bible. In the space below, I am going to list every verse in the Bible that mentions infant baptism:

_____

_____

Got it? The Bible never teaches or even hints that we are to baptize infants.

Baptism is an outward expression of an inward transformation. A young child has not yet experienced that inward transformation.

Baptism shows the world that you have been saved; it does not save you.

Dr. James Merritt says, "Because it represents the death, burial and resurrection of Christ, we believe biblical baptism must be by immersion. As we see in the New Testament, every baptism was by immersion, including the baptism of Jesus. In the Greek New Testament (the original language of the New Testament), the word for baptize is baptizo, which means to submerge or dip under water."[18]

THE "HOW" OF BAPTISM

To learn the how of baptism, let's look at a baptism story from the book of early church:

Now as they went down the road, they came to some water. And the eunuch said, "See, here is water. What hinders me from being baptized?" Then Philip said, "If you believe with all your heart, you may." And he answered and said, "I believe that Jesus Christ is the Son of God." (Acts 8:36–37)

Here is the first lesson from this passage: baptism is not a cause of salvation. Believing precedes baptism. New birth precedes baptism. You can be saved without being baptized, and the thief on the cross is the prime example.

Baptism does not save. It identifies who has been saved. It is like my wedding ring. If I take off my wedding ring, I am still married. My wedding ring does not make me married. My wedding ring identifies me as a married man.

But the symbol is important. If I told my wife that I was going on a trip and I didn't want people to know that I was married and was leaving my wedding ring at home… that would be a problem. The person who professes Christ but does not want to publicly identify himself as a follower of Christ… that is a problem.

The second "How" of baptism is this: baptism is by immersion. Notice what this passage says about the water:

So he commanded the chariot to stand still. And both Philip and the eunuch went down into the water, and he baptized him. Now when they came up out of the water, the Spirit of the Lord caught Philip away, so that the eunuch saw him no more; and he went on his way rejoicing. (Acts 8:38–39)

Why did they stop the chariot and go down into the water to be baptized? Because New Testament baptism is always by immersion. It is what the word means. One Greek dictionary explains that the word means "to dip. Immerse, submerge… to overwhelm, saturate."[19]

There is an interesting example of this in Mark 7:4. Note the words wash and washing. In both cases, the underlying Greek word is baptizo. "When they come from the marketplace, they do not eat unless they wash. And there are many other things which they have received and hold, like the washing of cups, pitchers, copper vessels, and couches" (Mark 7:4).

Now, I want to invite you to think about what they did with those cups and pitchers and vessels in order to clean them. How do you clean your dishes? (Imagine you don't have a dishwasher.) Do you sprinkle water on your dishes to get them clean? No, you immerse them.

This is another example of a truth we saw in the last chapter. Nearly every word that we think of as a religious word was originally just a normal word. In the last chapter, we saw that saved was not originally a theological word. It was just an ordinary word that meant to help.

The word for baptize—baptizo—was just an ordinary word as well. It was not a religious word about a religious ritual. It was a normal word, and it never meant sprinkle. It always meant immerse.

I love this story:

A boy went to church without his parents. When he got home, his mom asked him about it. He described the baptism that he saw. He said the preacher got into the water, held up his hand, and said, "I baptize you in the name of the Father, and the Son, and in the hole you go."

Baptizo was used in the ancient world to describe the process of taking a cloth and dipping it in dye. It describes how we wash dirty dishes. We have examples in the ancient world where the word was used to describe a boat sinking. To baptize simply means "to go under the water."

This is not just a Baptist doctrine; it is acknowledged by people who don't even practice baptism by immersion. For example, Martin Luther, founder of the Lutheran church, said, "I could wish that the baptized should be totally immersed according to the meaning of the word."[20]

Philip Schaff (Presbyterian): "Immersion, and not sprinkling, was unquestionably the original, normal form."[21]

John Calvin (Presbyterian): "It is evident that the term baptize means to immerse, and that this was the form used by the primitive Church."[22]

George Whitefield (Methodist): "It is certain that the words of our text is an allusion to the manner of baptism by immersion."[23]

You might be thinking, "Isn't sprinkling just as good?" I say "no" for two reasons:

- *Immersion follows the biblical method.* It says of John that he baptized in Aenon because there "was much water there" (John 3:23). Speaking of Jesus' baptism, Mark records that he "came up out of the water" (Mark 1:10). The biblical pattern is always immersion.

- *Immersion presents the biblical message.* Immersion is a picture of the death, burial, and resurrection of Jesus. Going under the water is a picture of burial. Coming out of the water is a picture of being resurrected to a new way of life. Buried is the old self. Resurrected is the new man.

If you change the method, you change the meaning. Pouring, sprinkling, or splashing do not picture the death, burial, and resurrection of Jesus.

Suppose I got out my wallet, and you saw a picture of a woman in my wallet. You looked closely and realized that was not the picture of my wife but some other woman. Imagine that you asked me about it, and I said, "Oh, that is the picture that came with the wallet. I thought it was pretty, so I just left it in the wallet." Would you think that strange?

My wife would find it more than strange. She would find it highly offensive and hurtful. Pictures matter. The right picture matters. Having the wrong picture in baptism is an offense to the Christ who bought our salvation with His death, burial, and resurrection.

THE "WHY" OF BAPTISM

We are not baptized to be saved; we are baptized because we are saved. It is an outward representation of an inner reality.

Baptism does not wash away your sin. There is no soap in our baptistery to get dirt off the outside of your body. Only faith in the shed blood of Jesus can wash away your sin.

You could be baptized so many times you start to look like a raisin, and it would not wash away your sin. You could be baptized so many times in a cow pond that the tadpoles know you by name, and it would not wash away your sin. Jesus will gladly wash away your sin. Just ask Him. No baptism required.

BAPTISM ESTABLISHES WHO IS LORD

"No baptism required?"

You might be thinking you will just opt out of baptism. Let me invite you to keep thinking.

Baptism was the first thing Jesus asked of his followers:

> *Go therefore and make disciples of all the nations, baptizing them in the name of the Father and of the Son and of the Holy Spirit. (Matthew 28:19)*

How can you claim that you are following Christ if you refuse to do the first thing He asked you to do? Baptism is not an option. It is not an elective. It is our first Christian duty.

It is a duty, but it is more than a duty. It is a delight. When you love someone, you are happy to let the world know. When I fell in love with my wife, I was happy to let the world know. It is not merely a duty for me to let the world know that I am married by wearing my wedding ring. It is my delight.

THE BENEFIT OF A SURRENDERED LIFE

You may be thinking that you would like salvation without Lordship. You would like to go to Heaven when you die, but you would rather not surrender to Christ as Lord now. You don't want to go to Hell, but you don't want to live as a slave of Christ either.

The question as to whether or not this is possible has raised quite a stir in the theology world in recent years. John MacArthur and others have written a number of books defending the idea that it is impossible to accept Christ as Savior and not surrender to Christ as Lord. Others have written books attempting to refute MacArthur.

The central question is this: what do you believe about God? Do you believe that God is good? Do you believe that God is a rewarder (Hebrews 11:6)? Do you believe He is a God who is out to harm you or to help you? Do you believe that His commands are given "so that it may go well with you"? "Therefore hear, O Israel, and be careful to observe it, that it may be well with you, and that you may multiply greatly as the LORD God of your fathers has promised you--'a land flowing with milk and honey'" (Deuteronomy 6:3).

The promises of scripture are breathtaking. God offers a life full of loving relationship where we know and experience and express God's love. He offers us a worry-free life where we experience the peace that passes all understanding (Philippians 4:6-7). He offers a life full of joy, unspeakable joy. He offers a life free of guilt. He offers a life lived on purpose. Do you want that life?

Jesus' purpose in coming was not just to get you to Heaven when you die. It includes that, but His purpose is also to bring Heaven here on earth. That is why Jesus taught us to pray this:

Your kingdom come. Your will be done
On earth as it is in heaven.
(Matthew 6:10)

Jesus' purpose is, in the words of John Ortberg, that up there (Heaven) would come down here. Your life will never be perfectly Heaven, but it can be substantially more joyous, at peace, purposeful, loving, and so forth. Do you want that life?

That life is always lived on the other side of the door called "Lordship." You cannot lay hold of the John 10:10 abundant Christian life without letting go of the steering wheel of your life and leaving the driving to Jesus.

If you refuse to be baptized, it calls into question whether or not you have let go of the wheel. More than that, I question what you believe about God— do you believe that He is good? Do you believe that He is a rewarder? Do you believe that it is always in your best interest to live the Christian life?

SO WHAT?

Whenever we study the Bible, we do well to always ask, "So what?" What is the application? What are we to do about what we have studied? I'd like to close this chapter with a question of application for three groups of people. Perhaps you are:

- Saved but never baptized.
- Saved but never been immersed.
- Saved but baptized before salvation.

In all these cases, I'd invite you to joyfully follow Christ in the celebration of believer's baptism. What are you waiting for?

3

SPIRITUAL WARFARE

Ephesians 6

There is a war going on. Did you know? When you got saved, you got a bull's eye on your back. The devil is out to steal, kill, and destroy. I have had many people say to me that, when they got saved, things didn't get better; they got worse.

The Christian life is not a playground; it is a battleground.

Vance Havner used to say, "Casual Christians know nothing of spiritual warfare."[24] The fatal fact of the matter is that he is right; the average Christian today knows little about spiritual warfare.

The Bible says that we are not to be ignorant of Satan's devices (2 Corinthians 2:11). Yet, most Christians know almost nothing about the Devil, his demons, his strategies, his strongholds, and (most importantly) how to overcome the evil one. What would be your chances of winning a war if you didn't even know the war was going on?

In the introduction to *The Screwtape Letters*, C.S. Lewis said, "There are two equal and opposite errors into which our race can fall about the devils. One is to disbelieve in their existence. The other is to believe and to feel an excessive and unhealthy interest in them. They themselves are equally pleased by both errors and hail a materialist or a magician with the same delight."²⁵ Which error do you think Christians more commonly fall into? What about you?

We need to learn how to analyze our enemy, utilize our weaponry, and maximize our victory. That is what it means to war and to win the battle. A key passage on this follows:

> *Finally, my brethren, be strong in the Lord and in the power of His might. Put on the whole armor of God, that you may be able to stand against the wiles of the devil. For we do not wrestle against flesh and blood, but against principalities, against powers, against the rulers of the darkness of this age, against spiritual hosts of wickedness in the heavenly places. Therefore take up the whole armor of God, that you may be able to withstand in the evil day, and having done all, to stand. Stand therefore, having girded your waist with truth, having put on the breastplate of righteousness, and having shod your feet with the preparation of the gospel of peace; above all, taking the shield of faith with which you will be able to quench all the fiery darts of the wicked one. And take the helmet of salvation, and the sword of the Spirit, which is the word of God. (Ephesians 6:10–17)*

WE ARE ENGAGED IN A SPIRITUAL WAR

It is a fact. You may not like it, but it is a fact. Wishing it were not so does not make it go away. Ignoring it does not make it disappear.

Verse 12 speaks of wrestling. The word is used only here in the New Testament. The word speaks of hand-to-hand conflict that involves both intense physical exertion and mental alertness. Wrestling was not a sport, as we think of it. Rather, wrestling was conflict with a real enemy—a bandit that might attack on a country road. John MacArthur says that in "fights in ancient Rome the conflict was real and often a matter of life for the winner and death for the loser."²⁶

The wrestling is in the spiritual realm. It is, perhaps, easier for us to think about multiple realities operating in the same space than it was for them. In the room where you are sitting right now exist all kinds of realities simultaneously. There is country and western music in the room. There is rock. There is talk radio. There are likely a few over-the-air TV shows. All you would need would be a device—a radio or

SPIRITUAL WARFARE

TV—to capture and display these realities that are already in the room where you read.

In a similar way, there is a spiritual reality in the room. And in that spiritual reality, we are at war. We may not like the idea. It may be a little creepy. But it doesn't take away from the fact that it is true. We are at war.

You may not hear physical bullets whizzing past you. You may not hear bombs blowing up around you, but the war in the spiritual realm is just as real as the realities of the physical realm.

This war is being fought in your home. This is why so many marriages are in trouble. It is why children are rebelling. It is why home is so often not a synonym for peace, comfort, security, and joy.

This war is being fought in your head. There is a battle for the mind. Christian living is won or lost in the mind. Abundant living is won or lost first in the mind, then in the life. Johnny Hunt says, "Satan would rather get you to think wrong than do wrong because if you think wrong, you will eventually do wrong."[27]

The war is being fought in your heart. It is being fought in your desires. If Satan can get you to want the wrong things, you will eventually do the wrongs things. Paul said he had learned to be content no matter what. There are an army of advertisers spending millions trying to make you discontent. Contentment is an issue of the heart. Not many of us have learned contentment. We can quote the twenty-third Psalm, but "I shall not want" has not become our reality.

The war is being fought in our world. The evidence is in every newspaper and on the nightly news every day. Every day we see murder and rape and prostitution and lying and cheating and stealing and terrorism and child molestation. This is the work of the evil one.

The Scripture says, "We do not wrestle with flesh and blood." This means that when I am in traffic and someone cuts me off, the little lady in the blue Honda Accord is not my enemy. I don't wrestle with flesh and blood.

We do not wrestle with flesh and blood, but we do wrestle. If you are a Christian, you are in the army now. There are no exceptions. There are no exemptions. There are no deferments. There are not conscientious objectors. If you are a Christian, your daily song should be "Onward Christian Soldiers" because you are at war.

God not only puts salvation in your heart; He puts a Sword in your hand. We have too many Christians that are asleep in the barracks and not out engaging the enemy. We have far too many Christians who have laid down their weapons and have surrendered without firing a shot.

If you don't run into the devil every morning, it means you are going in the same direction.

There is a war going on, and in this war, neutrality is not an option. C.S. Lewis said, "There is no neutral ground in the universe; every square inch, every split second, is claimed by God and counter-claimed by Satan."[28]

KNOWING THE ENEMY

Let's look at some of the names for Satan used in Scripture:

- *Satan* is used 54 times and means "adversary." He is our enemy. He is out to kill, steal, and destroy (John 10:10).
- *Devil* is used 35 times and means "slanderer." "Satan" is his name; "Devil" is his title. Slander is what he does. He criticizes. He belittles. He accuses.
- *Accuser of our brethren* (Revelation 12:10). This is what Satan does—accuses. It is his job. God convicts of sin and convinces us that we are loved. Satan accuses and condemns. Condemnation has no place in Christian living (Romans 8:1). The devil is all about condemnation.
- *Lucifer.* This was Satan's original name before the fall (Isaiah 14:12). The English word *Lucifer* comes from the Latin for "light bearer."[29] The Hebrew word means "morning star," and the NIV translates it with this phrase. It suggests that Satan's glory does not last long. The morning star is soon eclipsed by the sun.
- *Abaddon* (Revelation 9:11). It means "wound or destruction." This is what Satan does: destroys.
- *Apollyon* (Revelation 9:11). "One who destroys or corrupts."
- *Beelzebub* (Matthew 12:27). Based on the Hebrew for "Lord of the flies" or "Lord of manure pile."
- *The old serpent* (Revelation 20:2).
- *The Evil One* (John 17:15). Jesus prayed that the Father would protect us from the evil one.

SPIRITUAL WARFARE

- *The god of this age* (2 Corinthians 4:4). Paul says the god of this age has blinded the minds of unbelievers.
- *Father of lies* (John 8:44). Some speak English; others speak Spanish. Satan speaks lies. It is his native language. He has no real power other than deception. He is not an enemy with strong muscles so much as an enemy with smoke and mirrors. His method is deception.

Ephesians 6 reminds us that the devil is not the only thing we have to worry about:

For we do not wrestle against flesh and blood, but against principalities, against powers, against the rulers of the darkness of this age, against spiritual hosts of wickedness in the heavenly places. (Ephesians 6:12)

The Devil has, in all likelihood, never met you. He has never tempted you. He knows nothing about you. He has never bothered you. The Devil has demons who do his work. The Devil has far bigger fish to fry than you or me. Let's look at some of his minions:

- *Principalities.* This is the high order of demons. It is linked with "authorities" in Colossians 2:15. Most modern translations have it as "rulers." These are the generals of Satan's army. Some have suggested that these designations have geographical authority, so that there is a demon over America and a demon over Mexico and so forth. Others suggest that demons have areas of specialty—one group is in charge of lust while another instigates greed. (I am personally convinced that there are special demon forces in charge of technology. I am only about half kidding.)
- *Powers* is another rank in Satan's army—presumably one level down the chain of command.
- *Rulers of the darkness of this age.* Satan loves the darkness. He loves what is hidden. He loves what is secret. Nasty things grow in the darkness. Sin hides in secrecy.
- *Spiritual hosts of wickedness in heavenly places.* We are arrayed against a vast host of evil.

What this means is that your boss in not your adversary. That family member is not your adversary. The devil uses people, but people are not the enemy. We don't fight against flesh and blood.

We face a fierce enemy. In the great hymn, "A Mighty Fortress is Our God," Martin Luther wrote,

> *For still our ancient foe doth seek to work us woe; his craft and power are great, and armed with cruel hate, on earth is not his equal.*

His craft and power are great—but let's not overstate things. He is not like God. He is not omnipresent. He is not omniscient. He is not omnipotent. This is why he must operate through principalities and powers and spiritual hosts of wickedness. He can't do it all, so he gets his minions to do his dirty work.

Read this next sentence carefully: the devil is more like us than he is like God. God is infinitely powerful. The devil, like us, is limited. If you compare a BB to a bowling ball, the bowling ball is much bigger. But if you compare both of them to the known universe, they are both quite small by comparison. We and the devil are both small in comparison to God. It is in this sense that I say that the devil is more like us than he is like God.

I am afraid that many believers secretly believe in dualism—that is the idea that there are two more-or-less equal forces at play—God and the devil. The way some see it, God may be slightly more powerful, but the devil is going to give Him a run for His money. This is heresy.

THE ENEMY'S AMMUNITION

Ephesians 6:16 describes Satan's ammunition as fiery darts. What is a fiery dart?

A fiery dart is a thought.

A fiery dart is an unholy, unscriptural, demonic thought. It is a thought that is contrary to truth. It is a thought that we are told to take captive:

> *For though we walk in the flesh, we do not war according to the flesh. For the weapons of our warfare are not carnal but mighty in God for pulling down strongholds, casting down arguments and every high thing that exalts itself against the*

knowledge of God, bringing every thought into captivity to the obedience of Christ. (2 Corinthians 10:3–5)

Spiritual warfare is primarily fought between your ears. The battlefield is in your mind. Spiritual warfare is a battle to believe the truth. The Bible says, "For as he thinks in his heart, so is he" (Proverbs 23:7). The Bible says we are transformed by the renewing of our minds (Romans 12:2).

Spiritual warfare is a battle for your mind. It is a war for your thought life. It is a battle to lay hold of a truth-saturated way of thinking.

Notice the word *stronghold* in 2 Corinthians 10:4. A stronghold is an area of repeated failure. It is a place where a habit of thinking brings you repeated defeat. We tend to look of the outward defeat, but behind every outward defeat is an inward pattern of thinking.

A stronghold is built in five steps:

1. *It always begins with a thought.* How does Satan turn a man into a greedy, miserly, selfish man? It always begins with a thought. "I want that." "That will make me happy." "I deserve that." "I worked hard for what I have and am justified in spending it all on myself."

2. *The thought is repeated until it becomes a habit.* Martin Luther said, "You can't keep the birds from flying overhead but you can keep them from nesting in your hair."[30] When you think a thought over and over, it becomes a habit. You aren't even aware you are thinking it. Just as a fish does not know it is wet, you are thinking lies and do not know it. It has become your normal. It is not what you don't know that will hurt you; it is what you believe is so that ain't.

3. *We take action on the thoughts.* Thoughts have consequences. You can't keep thinking a thought over and over without eventually acting on it. This is why Jesus made the connection between lust and adultery. If you think lustful thoughts long enough, eventually, you will act on them. It is why Jesus connected anger and murder. If you harbor angry thoughts, bad things will happen.

4. *When the action is repeated, it becomes a habit.* Most of life is habit. Success in spiritual warfare is mostly about cultivating Christian habits. Good habits are hard to make and easy to

live with. Bad habits are easy to form but lead to destruction. People of prayer don't try really hard to pray every day; they pray out of habit. People who serve God don't try really hard to do the service they do; they serve out of habit. People who are consistently in the Word are not in the Word out of herculean effort to get the Book open every day; it is a habit. Success in life is largely about forming good habits and letting habits take care of us.

5. *The enemy forms the habit into a spiritual stronghold.* Think of a stronghold as an impenetrable fort. Daunting as it is, it is built one brick at a time. One activity at a time. One habit at a time.

    Suppose you have a stronghold in the area of lust or anger or materialism or gossip or complaining. How did it get there? One thought at a time; one action at a time. One habit at a time. How do you tear down that stronghold? One thought at a time; one action at a time; one habit at a time.

Ralph Waldo Emerson said,

Sow a thought and you reap an action; sow an act and you reap a habit; sow a habit and you reap a character; sow a character and you reap a destiny.

It all begins with a thought.

The devil will use anything he can to plant that thought in your mind. He might use a television commercial. He might use a magazine. He might use a song. He might use a TV program. He might use something you saw at the beach that you should not have looked at… twice.

Satan tends to be as efficient as possible. That is, he will tempt you with as little effort on his part as possible. He won't hit you on the head with a 2 X 4 when a twig will knock you off your feet.

Peter reminded us that we need to be vigilant. "Be sober, be vigilant; because your adversary the devil walks about like a roaring lion, seeking whom he may devour. Resist him, steadfast in the faith, knowing that the same sufferings are experienced by your brotherhood in the world" (1 Peter 5:8–9).

Perhaps Peter had in mind the hungry lions caged up underneath Rome's arenas and waiting to be released on helpless Christians. It is in

SPIRITUAL WARFARE

the nature of hungry lions to be always on the lookout for food. Satan is pictured standing, drooling at the mouth, watching for Christians whom he can lure away from the Lord.[31]

Satan is not playing games. He is out to devour you.

The root word translated *devour* actually means "to drink," not "to eat." Kittel says it means, "to gulp down."[32] It is translated other places as drown, swallow, or overwhelm. Think of how some animals swallow their prey whole; that is the picture here.

Satan wants to swallow you whole.

Think of this next time you want to dabble in sin. Remember this when you are tempted to nibble around the edges of some sin. You might be thinking, "A little is not a big deal." You have an enemy, and this is war. It is a big deal.

When the Allied forces landed at Normandy, they established a foothold on the continent of Europe. Historians tell us that once the beachhead was established, the war in Europe was over. It was the largest air, land, and sea operation undertaken before or since June 6, 1944. The landing included more than 5,000 ships, 11,000 airplanes, and more than 150,000 service men. The official end of the war did not come for nearly another year—May 8, 1945. But when the Allied forces took Normandy, it was over.

If Satan can get you started thinking about her and imagining being with her and lusting after her, the battle is lost, and you are defeated. It may be several months or years, but once the beachhead is established, the war is essentially over. This is why the Bible commands us to flee sexual immorality (1 Corinthians 6:18). It doesn't say to stand and resist. It says to flee. Run.

Are you ready for some good news?

WE ARE EQUIPPED WITH SPIRITUAL WEAPONS

Notice what Paul says about our weapons:

> *For the weapons of our warfare are not carnal but mighty in God for pulling down strongholds. (2 Corinthians 10:4)*

What are these weapons? The come in two categories. First, there are defensive weapons:

- *Belt of Truth.* Satan is the Father of Lies. We combat his attacks with a thorough knowledge of truth. Satan is out to deceive.

When he lies, he speaks his native language. The Christian warrior must be equipped with truth.

- *Breastplate of Righteousness.* "For He made Him who knew no sin to be sin for us, that we might become the righteousness of God in Him" (2 Corinthians 5:21). The Christian warrior looks at himself in the mirror every day and says, "In Christ, I am altogether righteous." Satan is out to deceive; he is also out to accuse. He is out to condemn. Those thoughts of what a dirty rotten person you are don't come from God. You are a sinner, but God has greater grace. Receive His grace, and take on the Breastplate of Righteousness.

- *Having shod your feet with the preparation of the gospel of peace.* These are shoes that help you move. Kent Hughes explains:

  > The image Paul has in mind comes from the Roman soldier's war boot, the caliga or half-boot which the legionnaire regularly wore while on duty. It was an open-toed leather boot with a heavily nail-studded sole which was tied to the ankles and shins with straps. These were not shoes for running—for example, fleeing or pursuing an enemy. In fact, Josephus tells of a centurion who, because he was running after his enemies while wearing "shoes thickly studded with sharp nails," slipped and fell on his back on the stone pavement, where he was duly dispatched. These boots served for marching, especially in battle. Their function was like today's cleated football shoe. They gave the foot traction and prevented sliding. Much ancient battle was hand-to-hand and foot-to-foot, like on the line of scrimmage, so these boots gave the Roman soldier an advantage over ill-equipped foes. The "readiness" of our text pictures us being ready with our caliga firmly planted on solid ground. Thus established, the enemy is not going to be able to push us back. Rather, we are set to advance.[33]

- *Shield of Faith.* "The word Paul uses is not that for the comparatively small round shield; it is that for the great oblong shield which the heavily armed warrior wore. One of the most dangerous weapons in ancient warfare was the fiery dart. It was a dart dipped in pitch. The pitch-soaked tip was set alight, and the dart was thrown. The great oblong shield was made of two sections of wood, glued together. When the shield was presented to the dart, the dart sank into the wood and the flame was put out. Faith can deal with the darts of temptation. With Paul, faith is always complete trust in Christ. When we walk close with Christ, we are safe from temptation."[34]
- *Helmet of Salvation.* "Satan wants to attack the mind, the way he defeated Eve (Genesis 3; 2 Corinthians 11:1–3). The helmet refers to the mind controlled by God. It is too bad that many Christians have the idea that the intellect is not important, when in reality it plays a vital role in Christian growth, service, and victory. When God controls the mind, Satan cannot lead the believer astray. The Christian who studies his Bible and learns the meaning of Bible doctrines is not going to be led astray."[35]

A Christian that does not take time every day to put on the belt, shoes, breastplate, and helmet is leaving himself open to our powerful enemy's attacks. He is in great danger of being destroyed. Adrian Rogers used to tell us that he physically stood in his closet and said, "OK, I am putting on that belt. I am slipping into those shoes. I am protecting my mind with the helmet. I am lifting that shield into place." We would all do well to do the same.

If you will put on the whole armor of God every single day, there is nothing that will come into your life that can separate you from the love of God.

God has given you awesome defensive weapons, but it doesn't stop there. He has also given you an awesome offensive weapon: the *Sword of the Spirit*, which is the Word of God (Ephesians 6:17).

My little boy is all boy. He can take anything and turn it into a sword. He loves to take a stick or a mop and turn it into a sword. Jack loves to pick up a sword. We would all do well to be like Jack.

The Sword of the Spirit is the Word of God. This reminds us if we are going to withstand the fiery darts of the enemy, we must be people of the Book. We must be people who start our day with our Bible on our lap. We must be people who memorize the Word and meditate on the Word and, most importantly, apply the Word. There is no other way to attack the enemy.

The enemy will send a fiery dart of lust, and all you have to do is get out the verse that says, "But I say to you that whoever looks at a woman to lust for her has already committed adultery with her in his heart" (Matthew 5:28).

The enemy will send a fiery dart and tempt you to discontentment. Get out the verse that says, "Not that I speak in regard to need, for I have learned in whatever state I am, to be content" (Philippians 4:11).

God will call you to do something, and the devil will tempt you to believe you can't do it. Pick up your Shield and quote, "I can do all things through Christ who strengthens me" (Philippians 4:13).

The devil will tempt you to worry. This verse has come to my aid many times, "Be anxious for nothing, but in everything by prayer and supplication, with thanksgiving, let your requests be made known to God; and the peace of God, which surpasses all understanding, will guard your hearts and minds through Christ Jesus" (Philippians 4:6–7).

WE WILL EXPERIENCE SPIRITUAL VICTORY

As believers, we do not fight for victory, we fight from victory. The battle has already been won; we just have to claim the victory. Jesus won the battle. Jesus won the war. Jesus claimed the victory at the cross.

All we have to do is learn to walk in the realization of that victory. Paul describes this victory in the first chapter of Ephesians:

> *…that the God of our Lord Jesus Christ, the Father of glory, may give to you the spirit of wisdom and revelation in the knowledge of Him, the eyes of your understanding being enlightened; that you may know what is the hope of His calling, what are the riches of the glory of His inheritance in the saints, and what is the exceeding greatness of His power toward us who believe, according to the working of His mighty power which He worked in Christ when He raised Him from the dead and seated Him at His right hand in the heavenly places, far above all principality and power and might and dominion, and every name that is named, not only in this*

SPIRITUAL WARFARE

age but also in that which is to come. And He put all things under His feet, and gave Him to be head over all things to the church, which is His body, the fullness of Him who fills all in all. (Ephesians 1:17–23)

When Jesus came out of the tomb, he claimed the victory. Everything is under His feet. Everything is under His control. He is Lord of all. There is a throne in Heaven, and Jesus is seated on it (Revelation 4:2). God is sitting on the throne. He isn't pacing the floor in worry. God is sitting confidently on His throne. As a saint in Christ, you can claim the victory.

John said, "He who is in you is greater than he who is in the world" (1 John 4:4). He who is in you is greater than your addiction. He who is in you is greater than your habits. He who is in you is greater than your hang ups. You can live in spiritual victory.

If you are defeated spiritually, there is one and only one reason. You are not taking up the spiritual armor that He has provided. You can live in victory. There are strongholds, and they will take some effort to take down. But they can be taken down. They can be defeated. You can be victorious.

You can walk in the fullness of the Spirit. You can live the John 10:10 abundant Christian life. You can lay hold of the spiritual victory that is ours in Christ. The victory is yours. Lay hold of it.

I heard the story of a German prison camp at the end of World War II. The American prisoners had gotten ahold of a small radio, and on it they heard the news that the war was over and America had won. But they were still in a prison camp. In that prison camp, this news changed everything.

Those captives spent the next three days whooping and hollering and yelling and cheering. There was laughter and back-slapping and hugs and tears. In a way, nothing had changed. They were still prisoners in a German prison camp. But, in a profound way, everything had changed. The victory had been won.

We are a lot like those prisoners. The circumstances of our lives may not have changed all that much. But the news of victory changes everything. Walk in that victory.

4

ROOTED IN THE WORD

Psalm 119

Being rooted in the Faith is largely about spending time in the Word. We are transformed by the renewing of our minds. Only the Word of God can transform the mind. Only spending time reading, memorizing, meditating, and applying the Word of God will change a soul.

We are promised abundant life in John 10:10. The Bible says the fruit of walking in the Sprit is a life of love, joy, peace, longsuffering, kindness, goodness, faithfulness, gentleness, and self-control (Galatians 5:22-23). Who doesn't want that life?

We lay hold of the abundant, John 10:10 fruit of the Spirit life by spending time in the Word.

You will never be a growing Christian without spending time in the Word. You will never mature until you get into the Book and get the Book into you.

I love this old poem:

*These have God married
and no man shall part
Dust on the Bible
and drought in the heart*[36]

My dad wrote a quote from D.L. Moody on the inside of my ordination Bible, "This Book will keep you from sin, or sin will keep you from this Book."

Howard Hendricks tells the story of a man who came to hear him teach at a Bible conference. The man complimented him, saying he and his family had driven all the way across the country just to be under the Word of God.

Dr. Hendricks began to reflect on that conversation. He wondered if the man who drove all the way across the country to sit under the Word of God is willing to walk across the room, pick up a Bible, and get in the Word of God.

We have churches full of people who come to church to sit under the Word of God. Good for them. I wonder how many will get in the Word of God on their own. George Barna reports that, "Only 37% of Americans report reading the Bible once a week or more."[37]

AS MUCH AS RICHES

The longest chapter in the Bible is Psalm 119, and it is about the Bible. The Psalm gushes with appreciation for the Word of God...

- "Your word I have hidden in my heart, that I might not sin against You" (Psalm 119:11).
- "I have rejoiced in the way of Your testimonies. As *much as* in all riches" (Psalm 119:14).
- "I will delight myself in Your statutes; I will not forget Your word" (Psalm 119:16).
- "Your testimonies also *are* my delight *and* my counselors" (Psalm 119:24).
- "Make me walk in the path of Your commandments, for I delight in it" (Psalm 119:35).
- "The law of Your mouth *is* better to me than thousands of *coins of* gold and silver" (Psalm 119:72).

Psalm 119 is an acrostic. There are twenty-two sections in the Psalm, each with eight verses. Each of the eight verses in the first section begins with the Hebrew letter "Aleph" (Think "A."). Each of the lines in the next section begins with "Beth" (Think "B.") and so on through the Psalm. Let's look at section one and part of section two:

Blessed are the undefiled in the way, Who walk in the law of the LORD!
Blessed are those who keep His testimonies, Who seek Him with the whole heart!
They also do no iniquity; They walk in His ways.
You have commanded us
To keep Your precepts diligently.
Oh, that my ways were directed To keep Your statutes!
Then I would not be ashamed,
When I look into all Your commandments.
I will praise You with uprightness of heart, When I learn Your righteous judgments.
I will keep Your statutes;
Oh, do not forsake me utterly!
How can a young man cleanse his way? By taking heed according to Your word.
With my whole heart I have sought You;
Oh, let me not wander from Your commandments!
Your word I have hidden in my heart, That I might not sin against You.
(Psalm 119:1–11)

This Psalm teaches us not only how to get into our Bible; it teaches how to get the Bible into us.

Determine Why

With a strong enough "why," the "how" tends to take care of itself.

If you want to lose weight, you need a strong why. You need to be convinced that you will feel better, live longer, and glorify God by taking good care of His temple. If you merely think that losing weight would be nice, you will never lose the weight and keep it off. Tell yourself, "Nothing tastes as good as fit feels."

If you want to get out of debt and stay out of debt, you need a big why. There are lots of little reasons why you would like to buy this or that instead of paying off debt. Tell yourself, "No purchase makes me as happy as being out of debt feels."

If you want to get into the Word and stay in the Word, you need a big reason why. You need to approach it like your life depends on it. Your spiritual life does. You may have started a plan of reading the Bible in the past but just couldn't stay with it. I am curious—why did you want to read the Word? Did you have a big honkin' WHY? To be consistent in reading the Word, you will need a big honkin' WHY.

In the last chapter, we looked at the fact that there is a real devil who is out to kill, steal, and destroy. He will do everything in his power to keep you from the Word. If you don't have a big honkin' WHY, the devil will win.

If your reason for getting into the Word is something like "I know that I need to," you won't get into the Word. If your reason for getting into the Word is "I really should," you won't be successful.

Here are 12 reasons WHY you should get into the Word:

1. *You can get to know the God of the Bible.* Bible reading is not just about being able to win a Bible trivia game. It is about getting to know the God of the Bible. God invites you into a daily, intimate relationship with Him. We do that through His Word. The old hymn writer said, "He walks with me and talks with me and tells me I am His own." He talks to us primarily through His Word.

2. *You read the Bible for transformation more than information.* As you read the Bible, you will be changed. Your life will get better. It won't happen in a day, but over time you will find that life is better as you spend time in the Word each day. As you read the Word, you want to look for how it applies to your life. You want to be a doer of the Word, not a hearer only (James 1:22). The Bible says, "As newborn babes, desire the pure milk of the Word, that you may grow thereby" (1 Peter 2:2).

3. *You read your Bible so that you can be used mightily by God.* God can use you even if you are a layman. God can use you even if you are old. God can use you even if you don't have a lot of gifts. God will never use you if you don't spend time in His Word. Bible study is the primary means that you prepare yourself to be an effective servant of God. There is an old saying: success is preparation meeting opportunity. Preparation for the spiritual battle is learning to use the Sword of the Spirit which is the Word of God (Ephesians 6:17).

4. *You read your Bible so that you can resist temptation.* Would you like to sin less than you do? The Bible says, "Your word

I have hidden in my heart, that I might not sin against You" (Psalm 119:11). "Hidden" translates an old Hebrew word—*memorize*. This is how Jesus resisted the devil when He was tempted in the wilderness. Three times the devil tempted, and three times Jesus countered with "It is written" (Matthew 4:4, 7, 10).

5. *You read your Bible so that you can gain wisdom.* The Bible places an extremely high value on wisdom. Solomon said, "Get wisdom! Get understanding! Do not forget, nor turn away from the words of my mouth" (Proverbs 4:5). Wisdom will make your life better. I like this old saying, "It is not what you don't know that will hurt you. It is what you think is so that ain't so."

6. *You read your Bible so that you can be an example to others.* Do you want your kids to read the Word? Do you think fellow church members should be people of the Book? Be a positive example with your life. "Let your light so shine before men, that they may see your good works and glorify your Father in heaven" (Matthew 5:16). We are all profoundly influenced by the people in our lives. Your life influences others—especially the ones you are closest to. You might want to look for a "verse of the day" and post it on Facebook or other social media as an encouragement to others to read. Of course, motive is everything. In the same sermon where Jesus said, "Let your light so shine before men..." He also said, "Take heed that you do not do your charitable deeds before men, to be seen by them..." (Matthew 6:1).

7. *You read your Bible so you can be ready to share the good news.* The Bible teaches we are to be ever ready to share. "Always be ready to give a defense to everyone who asks you a reason for the hope that is in you, with meekness and fear" (1 Peter 3:15).

8. *You read your Bible to help conquer worry, doubt, and fear.* Do you ever struggle with worry? Imagine what a difference it would make in your life if you meditated on this verse every day. I love the way the *Living Bible* paraphrases this: "Don't worry about anything; instead, pray about everything; tell God your needs, and don't forget to thank him for his answers. If you do this, you will experience God's peace, which is far

more wonderful than the human mind can understand. His peace will keep your thoughts and your hearts quiet and at rest as you trust in Christ Jesus" (Philippians 4:6–7, The Living Bible).

9. *You read your Bible so that your family will be better than it is.* Every husband would do well to memorize and meditate on this verse: "So husbands ought to love their own wives as their own bodies; he who loves his wife loves himself" (Ephesians 5:28). Every wife would be a better wife if she daily meditated on these words: "Let the wife see that she respects her husband" (Ephesians 5:33).

10. *You read your Bible because it is a flat-out interesting book.* The Bible is the world's best seller—every year. It has been estimated that it has sold six trillion copies. (A book that sells 100,000 copies will proudly proclaim it on the cover. 100,000 copies is relatively rare.) It has been translated into more than a thousand languages. It is the Bible's interestingness that David had in mind when he wrote, "How sweet are Your words to my taste, Sweeter than honey to my mouth!" (Psalm 119:103). Honey was the sweetest thing available back in the day. Today he might say, "Your Word is sweeter than a Krispy Kreme donut!"

11. *You read the Bible so that you can be prosperous and successful.* I wouldn't be comfortable saying it this way except that the Bible does: "This Book of the Law shall not depart from your mouth, but you shall meditate in it day and night, that you may observe to do according to all that is written in it. For then you will make your way prosperous, and then you will have good success" (Joshua 1:8). One more: "But his delight is in the law of the LORD, and in His law he meditates day and night. He shall be like a tree Planted by the rivers of water, That brings forth its fruit in its season, Whose leaf also shall not wither; And whatever he does shall prosper" (Psalm 1:2-3). The Bible's view of success is different from the world's. The world's view of success can be summarized in one word: money. The biblical view is broader. It has to do with the Shalom of God resting with you. It is the idea that life is as it should be. It is being rich in peace, and love, and relationships, and purpose.

12. *You read the Bible as an act of obedience.* Somewhere along the line we come to the point where we realize that God is God and we are not. If He commands me to spend time in the Word, I will obey.

Pick a Place for Bible Reading

Jesus said to go to your closet and close the door. It doesn't have to be a closet, although it could be. During college, Andy Stanley created a prayer closet underneath the stairs in the basement of his parent's house. In his case, it really was a closet.

It doesn't have to be a closet, but it does need to be a place where you can be alone. It needs to be a place where you will not be disturbed or distracted.

For Susanna Wesley, finding a prayer closet was a bit of a challenge:

> *Susanna Wesley, the mother of John and Charles Wesley, had nineteen children. She was committed to solitude. In the middle of her busy day, she would pull her apron up over her head and have her quiet time. When the apron went up, the children knew mom was praying and reading her Bible and they left her alone.*[38]

Sometimes, finding a place to be alone can be a challenge, especially for mothers of young children. Researchers once surveyed people about their favorite room in the house. The top answer was the kitchen. People love that one. Most husbands' top answer was the bedroom. Want to guess what the top answer was for mothers of young children?

The bathroom. Alone at last.[39]

For some of us, it is a challenge to find a place to be alone. If you want a life-changing time in the Word, you have to find a place to be alone.

The Bible says about Jesus, "Now in the morning, having risen a long while before daylight, He went out and departed to a solitary place; and there He prayed" (Mark 1:35). The place of prayer mattered to Jesus.

The "When" of Bible Reading

The where and the when are related. Notice that for Jesus it was "long before daylight." If you get up long before daylight, it might open up some places that would not work two hours later.

The Bible says about Abraham, "And Abraham went early in the morning to the place where he had stood before the LORD" (Genesis 19:27).

For most people, morning works best. But, if you are not a morning person, you might find some other time that works well. There are three key things to selecting time to spend in the Word:

- It must be an undistracted time. It must be free from interruptions.
- It must be a time when you are at your best. Don't give God your left-over time. God rarely speaks to me when I am sleepy. God rarely speaks to me before my morning coffee. Give God a time when you are alert.
- It must be an unhurried time.

Hurry is the great enemy of spiritual maturity. John Ortberg tells of learning this from Dallas Willard:

> *Many years later I had moved to Chicago. Entering into a very busy season of ministry, I called Dallas to ask him what I needed to do to stay spiritually healthy. I pictured him sitting in that room as we talked. There was a long pause—with Dallas there was nearly always a long pause—and then he said slowly, "You must ruthlessly eliminate hurry from your life."*
>
> *"Okay, Dallas," I responded. "I've got that one. Now what other spiritual nuggets do you have for me? I don't have a lot of time, and I want to get all the spiritual wisdom from you that I can."*
>
> *"There is nothing else," he said, generously acting as if he did not notice my impatience. "Hurry is the great enemy of spiritual life in our day. You must ruthlessly eliminate hurry from your life."*[40]

ROOTED IN THE WORD

I have one more John Ortberg insight, and it has to do with the topic of "when." What are you to do if you are not a morning person?

But what if morning is your worst time of the day? You may be the kind of person even Jesus doesn't want to talk to in the morning. Give him your best time. God created all kinds of people. Not all of them are morning prayers. "God made many other birds beside the larks."[41]

The Bible does not command us to get up early in the morning. In fact, the wisest man who ever lived said, "It is vain for you to rise up early, to sit up late, to eat the bread of sorrows; for so He gives His beloved sleep" (Psalm 127:2).

Some people are night owls. Some love to get up early. It is not *when* you spend time with God so much as *that* you spend time with God.

I am often asked how much time you should spend. Here is a real key: it does not matter the amount of time so much as the consistency of time.

Christianity is about a love relationship. Remember when you were first in love? When it came to spending time with that one you were all googly-eyed over—which was better: fifteen minutes or an hour? The same goes with your time with Jesus.

Suppose you talked to a young man who was considering getting in a relationship. He wanted to do right in the relationship, and he asked you, "How much time am I obligated to spend with a woman?" The truth is, if it is a big obligation, no amount of time is enough.

Again, consistency is more important than quantity. Here is what I recommend:

- *Set a low bar.* Set the goal of opening the Book every day. Set the goal of at least one chapter in the Word every day.
- *Allow for no exceptions.* If you plan to read the Bible every other day, it might always be an "other" day.

If you want to be rooted in Christ, there is no substitute for spending time in the Word. If you want to lay hold of the John 10:10 life, there is no substitute for spending time in the Word. I heard someone say, "That idea of having a quiet time is kind of old fashioned; it is so 90s. Do you have any innovative, modern ways to connect with God?"

No.

Spending time in the Word may be simple. It may be old-fashioned. You may have heard it before. But there is no substitute. There is no alternative. If you want to be hip and modern you can read the Bible on an iPad instead of a paper book, but you must spend time in the Word. Research bears out what the Bible teaches on this:

> *The findings presented in Unstuck are based on data from more than seventy thousand Americans who completed surveys between 2005 and 2011. Some surveys focused on specific groups; e.g., people who attend church regularly. Others draw from a random sample of the population. Regardless of which group we studied, in one regard the results were the same: Consistently engaging the Bible made a marked difference in people's spiritual lives.*[42]

How do we do spend time in the Word? What exactly, specifically, are we to do?

"HOW" TO SPEND TIME IN THE WORD

Let's imagine you set your alarm fifteen minutes early tomorrow morning to spend time in the Word. What do you do?

Study It Cleanly

God never pours fresh insight into an unclean vessel. Begin your time with God by confessing your sin.

The Bible says that if we confess our sin, God is faithful and just and will forgive our sin (1 John 1:9). The Greek word translated "confess" is a combination of two Greek words that mean "to say the same thing as." It means to admit that I am sinner. It is to see myself as God sees me.

Here is a paradoxical question: does the Bible have a high or low view of man? As we grow in Christ will we come to think more or less of ourselves? Is our problem thinking too much or too little of ourselves?

As we grow in Christ, we grow in a profound understanding of how deeply we are sinners. If you talk to someone who is far from God about this, he is likely to say that he is not that bad. Talk to someone who has been walking with Christ his entire life about his sin. They will say with Paul, "I am the chief of sinners." Growing in Christ is, in part, growing to understand how profoundly my sin has offended the heart of God.

But Christianity is not, as some have called it, "worm theology." The goal is not to think as badly as possible about yourself. Some seem to think that the more scummy they see themselves, the more spiritual they are. That is not the gospel.

The gospel is summed up in the words of a former slave trader. His name is John Newton, and he also penned the world's most famous hymn, *Amazing Grace*. John Newton said, "Though I have lost my memory, two things I know: I am a great sinner, and Christ is a great Savior."[43]

Take your sin seriously. God does. And take grace seriously. God forgives. Claim it. Receive it.

Study It Continuously

The best way to read the Bible is this: verse by verse; chapter by chapter; book by book. The worst way to study the Bible is to randomly select a chapter from a different place every day.

There is an old story about a guy that tried the second approach. He was at the end of his rope and didn't know what to do. So, he picked up the Bible and selected a random verse. The verse read, "Judas went out and hung himself" (Matthew 27:5).

That seemed a little puzzling. He was not sure what to do with that, so he decided to ignore it and try again. This time he turned to the verse that says, "Go and do likewise" (Luke 10:37).

Now, he was really confused. He decided to try one more time. So, he opened his Bible again and pointed to a verse. He looked down and found the verse that says, "What you do, do quickly" (John 13:27).

This is what happens when you read the Bible randomly. Read it sequentially. Start in a book and read through until you finish that book. Pick up tomorrow where you left off today.

You may not do it every year, but it is a great idea for every believer to read through the whole Bible using the *One Year Bible*. This Bible is available in various translations and divides the Bible into 365 daily readings. (You don't have to start on January 1.) Each reading has a Psalm, a Proverb, and a reading from the Old and New Testament. In twenty minutes a day, you can read through the whole Bible in a year.

I have heard the testimony of many who said their lives were changed when they did this.

Amos Wells once wrote,

> *I supposed I knew my Bible,*
> *Reading piecemeal, hit or miss,*
> *Now a bit of John or Matthew,*
> *Now a snatch of Genesis,*
>
> *Certain chapters of Isaiah,*
> *Certain Psalms (the twenty-third),*
> *Twelfth of Romans, first of Proverbs —*
> *Yes, I thought I knew the Word!*
>
> *But I found that thorough reading*
> *Was a different thing to do,*
> *And the way was unfamiliar*
> *When I read the Bible through.*
>
> *You who like to play at Bible,*
> *Dip and dabble, here and there,*
> *Just before you kneel, aweary,*
> *And yawn through a hurried prayer;*
>
> *You who treat the Crown of Writings*
> *As you treat no other book,*
> *Just a paragraph, disjointed,*
> *Just a crude, impatient look.*
>
> *Try a worthier procedure,*
> *Try a broad and steady view;*
> *You will kneel in very rapture*
> *When you read the Bible through.*[44]

I knew a man in a previous church that bore testimony to this. He dropped out of church for a long time—twenty years or more. This whole time he was not walking with God.

But, as God is prone to do, God didn't leave him alone. God got ahold of him. He began reading his Bible every morning. He started in January in Genesis. By July he had read the whole thing. He started again. Over the next few years, he read the Bible through over and over and over.

And I watched it right before my eyes: he began to change. He began to be a little more like Jesus. He began to worry less and love more. He began to be more joyful and less fearful. He became marked by the fruit of the Spirit. He was transformed by the renewing of His mind.

When you read God's Word, His Word will change you!

Study It Consistently

You wouldn't go a day without eating physical food; don't go a day without feasting from the bread of life.

Set a low bar—at least one chapter a day. No exceptions.

You can always read more. But never read less. And never miss a day. And, if you do miss a day, don't miss the next one.

This principle is applied to exercise, but it is not hard to adapt to spending time in the Word:

> *Think about exercise. I exercise every day, and I have for some time. But it wasn't an easy habit to establish in the beginning. Like a lot of well-intentioned people, I had made New Year's resolutions to go to the gym, but I always lasted for a few weeks, then failed. Then I listened to Woody Allen.*
>
> *Woody Allen famously said that 80 percent of the business of life is just showing up. It's a throwaway line, but it shows keen psychological insight and goes directly to the heart of default thinking. After many failed attempts at fitness, I made a vow to go to the gym every day. Just "show up"—no more. I found a gym that was reasonably convenient, so that wasn't a deterrent, then started putting on my sweats every morning and showing up. If I exercised, great, but if I didn't, that was okay too. I would at least make an appearance.*
>
> *You know what? I never once showed up without doing something, even if it was just hopping on the Stairmaster for twenty minutes. And it was almost always more, just because I was there, and why not? I was already sweaty. What I had done, without even realizing it at the time, was change my brain's default position. I had written a policy for myself, a policy that let my deliberating brain stay home while my automatic brain took over.*[45]

The key to spending time in the Word? Show up. The key to being transformed by the renewing of your mind? Show up. They key to living the John 10:10 abundant Christian life? Show up. Set a low bar—get the Book open. Allow for no exceptions.

Study It Carefully

Every believer should learn the art and science of how to study the Bible.

Every believer should be in the life-long practice of building a theological library. Start with some good Study Bibles—they contain a wealth of condensed information. Get some good Christian books.

Mark your Bible, and your Bible will mark you. Underline verses that stand out. Circle key words. Read with a highlighter in hand.

Occasionally pick up the Bible of an elderly saint who has been walking with God her whole life. You will find so many notes in the Bible, you will hardly be able to find the text itself. Every time she heard a sermon, she wrote notes in the Bible. Every page will have verses underlined. There will be arrows and stars and brackets and all kinds of hieroglyphs known only to that saint.

When I see a Bible like that, here is what I know: that is a saint who knows her Bible and knows her God.

William Coverdale produced a translation of the Bible that predates the King James and was basis for the King James Translation. In the flyleaf of his Bible, he wrote these words:

> *It shall greatly helpe ye to*
> *understand the Scripture,*
> *If thou mark*
> *Not only what is spoken or ritten,*
> *But of whom,*
> *And to whom,*
> *With what words,*
> *At what time,*
> *Where,*
> *To what intent,*
> *With what circumstances,*
> *Considering what goeth before and*
> *what followeth.*[46]

ROOTED IN THE WORD

Let me paraphrase this into twenty-first century terms: mark down what you see—that is observation. Mark down what it means—that is interpretation. Mark down how it works—that is application.

Study It Creatively

It is difficult for me to sit down for long periods of time. I have to get creative. I listen to the Bible so that I can walk around as I listen.

I visited Pastor Steve Gaines years ago when he was at Gardendale's First Baptist Church. I will never forget the blue carpet he had in his office. What struck me was not the carpet so much as the path worn in the carpet around the perimeter of that office. He had worn through the fabric of the blue carpet down to the tan fibers underneath. For hours every day, he would walk and read. For hours every day, he would walk and pray. Walk and read. Walk and pray. Until the blue carpet was worn to its tan underbelly.

If you would rather listen than read, here is some good news: you can read your Bible on your Smart Phone or have it read the Bible to you—all for free.

We have more and better tools for studying the Bible than any generation in history. You can get better tools on your smart phone than preachers a generation ago had in their libraries.

If you are studying Ephesians and would like to see what Ephesus looked like, Google it. In just a few clicks of the mouse, you will find stunning pictures. There are apps where, with just a few clicks, you can discover what the underlying Greek or Hebrew word is and how it is used elsewhere in the Bible. We have Bible apps for Scripture memory. We have better tools than any generation in history for studying the Bible. Take advantage of them.

Study It Corporately

Peter said, "No prophecy of Scripture is of any private interpretation" (2 Peter 1:20). Studying scripture is a deeply personal thing, but it is not a private thing. That is it is meant to be shared.

If you discover something in the Bible that doesn't make sense, ask a friend. Talk about what you read with your wife and kids. We ought to be constantly saying to one another, "Can I share with you the verse I read this morning?"

Nehemiah is an example of studying the Bible corporately. In Nehemiah 8, we read that Ezra read the Scriptures from a high pulpit they had built for that purpose. Then, people got in groups and studied what they had heard.

This is what we do in church today. We gather for a corporate worship service where the Word of God is preached. Then, we gather in small groups to further study and discuss the Word. If these groups meet on campus, we generally call this Sunday School, where there are classes for all ages from preschool to senior adults. Many churches are doing small group Bible study in homes these days. It doesn't matter so much *where* as it matters *that* we study the Bible with other believers.

If you want to be rooted in the Word, you need to be in a large group worship experience and a small group Bible study every week.

GETTING YOUR BIBLE INTO YOU

Getting into the Word is a start. The real point is to get the Word into you.

There was an Emperor in Ethiopia that ruled during the 1800s. His name was King Menelik II. When he would get sick, he took a page out of his Bible, tore it out, and ate it. He physically ate pages of the Bible. (Don't try this with your iPhone app.) I am told that before he died, he had eaten the entire book of 2 Kings. There is a better way!

The challenge is getting the Word from your head to your heart. We must go from information to transformation. The goal is not be become smarter sinners. It is not so much about what you learn, but what you live.

Dr. Steve Gaines calls it, "Learning to think Bible."

When something comes up in your life, what do you think first? A saying from your momma? Something your daddy told you? Advice from a secular self-help book? Or, does Scripture jump into your mind?

If you get into the Word every day and the Word gets into you, the Word becomes the first thing that comes to mind. This is what it means to think Christianly. This is what it means to "think Bible." This is what it means to be transformed by the renewing of your mind. How do you do that?

Memorization

"How can a young man cleanse his way? By taking heed according to Your word. Your word I have hidden in my heart, That I might not sin against You" (Psalm 119:9, 11). Would you like to sin less than you do? Hide God's Word in your heart. Memorize God's Word.

My kids participate in the Awana Program in our church. This program emphasizes Scripture memorization. I love to see my kids memorizing God's Word and getting it deep into their lives in the early years of their lives. It is my privilege as their dad to invest hours working with them and helping them hide God's Word in their hearts.

Bob Foster said that Scripture memory is "the daily habit of supplying the subconscious with God's material to chew on."[47]

I heard about a boy who was in a band. The band got invited to play on a Caribbean cruise. He knew there would be all kinds of alcohol and drunkenness, and he wanted to stay away from that. He had grown up in an alcoholic's home and saw firsthand the pain that comes from alcohol. He determined in his heart to stay away, but he knew that he would be tempted.

He memorized scripture that he might not sin against God. Sure enough, when he got on the boat, his fellow band members invited him to go get a drink. He quoted Proverbs 20:1, "Wine is a mocker, strong drink is a brawler, and whoever is led astray by it is not wise."

They still kept coming at him, tempting him to drink. He quoted Scripture, "At the last it bites like a serpent, and stings like a viper" (Proverbs 23:32).

Then, they got mad. They began to tease and mock and ridicule him. He quoted Scripture again. "My son, if sinners entice you, do not consent" (Proverbs 1:10).

Finally, one of the guys said, "Oh, leave him alone. He is so full of Scripture we can't do anything with him."

Memorizing Scripture will give you victory over sin. It will help you to overcome worry. It will give you confidence in sharing your faith. It will speed up the transformation process. It will help you discover God's will. It will equip you for service to God.

Contemplation

Contemplation means you meditate on what you memorize. I am not talking about sitting cross legged with your hands in the lotus position. It is not, as some say, about emptying your mind. It is about filling your mind with the truth of the Word of God and contemplating on what it says. John Ortberg says, if you can worry, you can meditate.[48]

Richard Foster says, "Christian meditation, very simply, is the ability to hear God's voice and obey His word."[49]

One way to do this is to go through a verse and emphasize one word at a time. For example, take John 15:7, "If you abide in Me, and My words abide in you, you will ask what you desire, and it shall be done for you."

- *If* — this suggests that it might or might not happen and whether or not it happens depends on me.
- *You* — insert your name here.
- *Abide* — dwell in; live in; be at home in. It means to hang out, not stop by occasionally.

Go through each word of the verse. You may not find meaning in every word, but you will in most of them.

Application

Put what you marked and memorized and meditated on into practice. Be a doer of the Word. Again, it is not about becoming a smarter sinner.

Bible study is about going from the heard, to the heart, to the hands. You only really believe what you obey.

- Do you believe it is good to give? Your checkbook will tell.
- Do you believe it is important to "forsake not the assembling of the saints"? Your calendar will tell.
- Do you believe it is good for you to forgive? Your bitterness or lack of will show what you believe.
- Do you believe it is good to serve others? When was the last time you served?

Discipleship is pretty simple, really. We read the Book. We study. We mark. We underline. We memorize. We meditate. Then, we do what it says to do.

- The Bible says to forgive, and we forgive.
- The Bible says to be kind, and we behave kindly.
- The Bible says to love, and we love.
- The Bible says to give, and we give.

Now, there is one more thing: we do all this in the power of the Holy Spirit. There is more to Christian living than trying really hard to be good.

Paul taught that Christian living is both active and passive: "To this end I also labor, striving according to His working which works in me mightily" (Colossians 1:29).

If we don't understand, "His working which works in me mightily," we will never lay hold of the John 10:10 life.

There was a wealthy vineyard owner who had two lazy, good-for-nothing, rotten boys. He knew that unless he did something drastic, they would lose everything when he died. So, just before he died, he told his boys that he had buried an immense fortune somewhere on the property.

For the next year, those boys spent every day on their hands and knees. They were on every square inch of that vineyard. They pulled up every weed. They tossed out every rock. At the end of the summer, they still hadn't found any treasure. They thought their father had lied.

Then the harvest came in. All that effort pulling weeds and removing rocks and caring for that vineyard began to pay off. They brought in the greatest harvest they had ever seen. Then it dawned on them: that was the treasure.

Our Heavenly Father has buried an immense treasure in the pages of the Bible. Dig it up for great profit.

You will find that you won't just carry your Bible; your Bible carries you.

You don't just read your Bible; your Bible reads you.

You don't just mark in your Bible; your Bible marks you.

Study the Bible to be wise.

Believe the Bible to be safe.

Practice the Bible to be holy.

Study it through.

Pray it in.

Work it out.

Note it down.

Pass it on.

5

ROOTED IN PRAYER

Luke 11:1–13

Jim Cymbala wrote:

The world has yet to see a Christlike, victorious, fruitful believer who was not a person of considerable prayer.[50]

William Carey wrote:

Prayer—secret, fervent, believing prayer—lies at the root of all personal godliness.[51]

If you are to become a godly Christian, you must become a person of prayer. There is no other way.

Still, many of us—including myself—feel inadequate in prayer. Perhaps you can relate to the confession of best-selling author, Max Lucado:

Hello, my name is Max. I'm a recovering prayer wimp. I doze off when I pray. My thoughts zig, then zag, then zig again. Distractions swarm like gnats on a summer night. If attention deficit disorder applies to prayer, I am afflicted. When I pray, I think of a thousand things I need to do. I forget the one thing I set out to do: pray.

Some people excel in prayer. They inhale heaven and exhale God. They are the SEAL Team Six of intercession. They would rather pray than sleep. Why is it that I sleep when I pray? They belong to the PGA: Prayer Giants Association. I am a card-carrying member of the PWA: Prayer Wimps Anonymous.[52]

I think the disciples could relate. That is why they asked Jesus how to pray. They never asked Jesus how to preach or heal. They did ask Jesus how to pray:

Now it came to pass, as He was praying in a certain place, when He ceased, that one of His disciples said to Him, "Lord, teach us to pray, as John also taught his disciples." (Luke 11:1)

I can relate to that question. Let me confess to you: I sometimes struggle with prayer. The tyranny of the urgent things in my life tends to crowd out the important things.[53] Sometimes my prayer life is not what it ought to be because the urgent ringing of the phone crowds out what is really important. It is no one's fault but my own.

An old saying goes, "If Satan can't make you bad, he will make you busy." Guilty as charged.

Sometimes I am tempted to believe that I don't matter to God and He has more to do than hear from me. I am tempted to believe that God doesn't really, really want to hear from little old me. Am I the only one?

It is possible for a high view of God to hinder our prayers. We think that God is so high and holy and separate and distant that we perceive God as not being interested in us. God is high and lifted up and holy and separate. But He is also intimate and acquainted with all of our ways. He is interested in everything we think and do. He cares about what we care about. He wants to hear from us.

If you are tempted to feel this way, let me remind you of a verse that has strengthened my heart many times:

O You who hear prayer, To You all flesh will come. (Psalm 65:2)

Literally the verse describes God as the "hearer of prayers." Hearing prayers is what God does. It is who He is. He is a God who hears prayers. You might begin your prayer that way, "Oh God, I come to you today because You are the hearer of prayers…"

You are not bothering God when you pray. He is delighted to hear from you. He doesn't have more important things to do. He can do everything all at once with half His intelligence tied behind His back. He is delighted to hear from His children as a good dad is delighted to hear from his kids.

God loves you. He is crazy about you. He longs for you. Zephaniah 3:17 says He sings over you. Picture a loving mother singing lullabies to her child as she sleeps. That is the picture we have of God's love for us. You are not disturbing God. He is not too busy for you.

God is a hearer of prayers, and He desires that we become people of prayers—prevailing, powerful, and personal prayers. In this chapter, we will look at five principles that will lead us to be people of prayer.

YOU MUST PRAY CONSISTENTLY

The Bible teaches that prayer was Jesus' norm. "So He Himself often withdrew into the wilderness and prayed" (Luke 5:16). The word "often" does not technically appear in the Greek. It is an attempt by the translators to communicate the tense of the Greek verb; the verb is in the imperfect, which is a linear tense in the Greek. It means this was Jesus' on-going practice. It was His habit.

For the believer, prayer is like breathing. You can go a little time without breathing. You can hold your breath for a short time. The record for longest time holding breath underwater was twenty-two minutes and zero seconds and was set by Stig Severinsen (Denmark) at the London School of Diving in London, UK, on May 3, 2012.[54]

You can hold your breath for a time, but you can't do so for long. And, if you want to live in communion with God, you can't live without prayer for long.

You learn to pray like you learn anything else—you learn by doing. You learn to pray by praying. We won't learn much at the rate we are going. According to George Barna, the average amount of time adults spend in prayer each day is about five minutes.[55]

Books on prayer can help, but the main thing is prayer. Teaching on prayer can help, but the main thing is prayer.

Do what Jesus did: "Now in the morning, having risen a long while before daylight, He went out and departed to a solitary place; and there He prayed" (Mark 1:35). Pick a time. Pick a place. Pray.

A day hemmed in prayer is unlikely to become unraveled.[56]

YOU MUST PRAY CORRECTLY

Jesus taught his disciples to pray, and through them, he taught all of us to pray. They saw something in His prayer life that they wanted.

I see six things in this model prayer that we can learn about praying correctly. Note that they spell the word prayer:[57]

P raise God

R epent of Your Sins

A sk for Yourself and Others

Y ield Yourself to God's Will

E xpect God's Answer

R epeat

Let's look at each of these six things.

Praise God

Prayer doesn't start with asking. Prayer starts with praising. "Hallowed be your name" means to recognize the holiness of God. Study the great prayers of the Bible, and you will discover they consistently start with praise.

The disciples are experiencing heavy persecution in Acts 4. Look at how the begin their prayer:

> *So when they heard that, they raised their voice to God with one accord and said: "Lord, You are God, who made heaven and earth and the sea, and all that is in them..." (Acts 4:24)*

Jehoshaphat was in trouble. He was surrounded by three armies. Here is how he starts his prayer:

> *O LORD God of our fathers, are You not God in heaven, and do You not rule over all the kingdoms of the nations, and in Your hand is there not power and might, so that no one is able to withstand You? (2 Chronicles 20:6)*

One more. Look at how David begins his prayer:

> *Therefore David blessed the LORD before all the assembly; and David said: "Blessed are You, LORD God of Israel, our*

Father, forever and ever. Yours, O LORD, is the greatness, The power and the glory, The victory and the majesty; For all that is in heaven and in earth is Yours; Yours is the kingdom, O LORD, And You are exalted as head over all. Both riches and honor come from You, And You reign over all. In Your hand is power and might; In Your hand it is to make great And to give strength to all. Now therefore, our God, We thank You And praise Your glorious name." (1 Chronicles 29:10–13)

The great prayers of the Bible consistently start the way Jesus told us to start our prayers: in praise.

What does this look like? I want to be very practical.

You might praise Him for saving and sealing you.
You might praise Him for healing and forgiving you.
You might praise Him for His blessings.
You might praise Him through His names…
He is Jehovah-Jireh, the Lord who provides.
He is Jehovah-Shalom, the Lord who is our peace.
He is Jehovah-Tsidkenu, the Lord our righteousness.
He is Jehovah-Rophe, the Lord who heals.
He is Jehovah-Mekadesh, the Lord who sanctifies.
He is Jehovah-Nissi, the Lord our banner.
He is Jehovah-Rohi, the Lord our shepherd.
He is Jehovah-Shammah, the Lord who is there.

In my prayer time this morning I began by praying through some of the names of Jesus…

You are the Lamb of God. You are the Great Shepherd.
You are the Light of the World. You are the Word.
You are the Door.
You are the Way, the Truth, and the Light.

The Bible says, "Enter into His gates with thanksgiving, And into His courts with praise. Be thankful to Him, and bless His name" (Psalm 100:4). Begin your prayer time with praise.

Another great way to praise is through music. We have access to great worship music today in every style imaginable. If the worship service you attend does not use exactly the musical style you prefer, I have some great news: you can make your own worship service in the privacy of your home. Just pop on some headphones or crank up the stereo and worship the Lord in song—loud song:

> *Praise Him with the sound of the trumpet;*
> *Praise Him with the lute and harp!*
> *Praise Him with the timbrel and dance;*
> *Praise Him with stringed instruments and flutes!*
> *Praise Him with loud cymbals;*
> *Praise Him with clashing cymbals!*
> *Let everything that has breath praise the LORD.*
> *Praise the LORD!*
> *(Psalm 150:3–6)*

Repent of Your Sins

When we come into the presence of God and we begin to worship and think about the holiness and purity of God, it is natural to think about our own sinfulness in comparison.

Spiritual growth is largely about deepening our understanding of the greatness, goodness, and holiness of God. This understanding causes us to realize how sinful we are in comparison. People who don't think much about God don't think they are all that bad. Thus, they don't have much need for grace.

This is the third step in spiritual growth:

1. Deepening our understanding of God.
2. Appreciating how profoundly we have violated the holiness of God.
3. Basking in the immensity of His amazing grace.

If we come to God with known, unconfessed sin, it creates a barrier between us and God. God will not hear our prayers. "But your iniquities have separated you from your God; and your sins have hidden His face from you, so that He will not hear" (Isaiah 59:2).

Jim Cymbala says, "It may be humbling to continually admit that we are helpless sinners saved by grace, but only this path will lead to a prayer-hearing God."[58]

When you try to come to God in your own righteousness, not admitting your sin, you are rejected. Let me say that again.

Rejected.

When you repent, He welcomes you with open arms.

There is line in an old hymn that admonishes us to count our many blessings, name them one by one. We do well to also name our sins one by one. We would do well to pray…

- God, I am materialistic and greedy. Cleanse my heart. Teach me to be content with all the blessings you provide.
- Lord, I worry when You told me not to worry. I confess my sinful worry. Empower my heart to trust you completely.
- Jesus, You told me to do everything without complaining and arguing. (Philippians 2:14, NIV) The truth is I complain all the time. I am sorry. I am wrong. Forgive me.
- God, my lustful heart is given to evil. Cleanse my heart, oh God.

"If we confess our sins, He is faithful and just to forgive us our sins and to cleanse us from all unrighteousness" (1 John 1:9). After you have confessed your sin, receive forgiveness. Claim forgiveness. Believe that you are forgiven. Take God at His Word. The evil one will try to condemn. The evil one will accuse. Don't listen to him. Confess, repent, and receive grace. Bask in grace. As they say in the South, waller in grace.

Ask for Yourself and Others

"Give us day by day our daily bread" (Luke 11:3).

This is where we come to God and ask for stuff. This is where we come to God and tell Him what our hopes, hurts, and fears are. This is where we ask for things for ourselves and others.

I have a question for you to consider: do you think our prayers are too big or too small? Do we, in our greed, ask for too much? Or, do we ask for too little?

Bruce Wilkinson tells a fable that suggests an answer to this question:

> *There's a little fable about a Mr. Jones who dies and goes to heaven. Peter is waiting at the gates to give him a tour. Amid the splendor of golden streets, beautiful mansions, and choirs of angels that Peter shows him, Mr. Jones notices an odd-looking building. He thinks it looks like an enormous warehouse—it has no windows and only one door. But when he asks to see*

inside, Peter hesitates. "You really don't want to see what's in there," he tells the new arrival.

Why would there be any secrets in heaven? Jones wonders. What incredible surprise could be waiting for me in there? When the official tour is over, he's still wondering, so he asks again to see inside the structure.

Finally Peter relents. When the apostle opens the door, Mr. Jones almost knocks him over in his haste to enter. It turns out that the enormous building is filled with row after row of shelves, floor to ceiling, each stacked neatly with white boxes tied in red ribbons.

"These boxes all have names on them," Mr. Jones muses aloud. Then turning to Peter he asks, "Do I have one?"

"Yes, you do." Peter tries to guide Mr. Jones back outside. "Frankly," Peter says, "if I were you...." But Mr. Jones is already dashing toward the "J" aisle to find his box.

Peter follows, shaking his head. He catches up with Mr. Jones just as he is slipping the red ribbon off his box and popping the lid. Looking inside, Jones has a moment of instant recognition, and he lets out a deep sigh like the ones Peter has heard so many times before.

Because there in Mr. Jones's white box are all the blessings that God wanted to give to him while he was on earth...but Mr. Jones had never asked.[59]

Although this is only a fable, I believe it tells an important truth: God wants to bless you. Here are the straightforward words from Jesus Himself, "Give, and it will be given to you: good measure, pressed down, shaken together, and running over will be put into your bosom. For with the same measure that you use, it will be measured back to you" (Luke 6:38).

Strictly speaking, this is a teaching on giving. But it teaches us something important about God: God loves to bless His people.

I believe our prayers are too small, not too big. Jesus taught us to pray, "Your kingdom come, Your will be done on earth as it is in heaven" (Matthew 6:10). He taught us to pray that earth would become like Heaven. Talk about a big prayer!

We tend to be interested in material or physical blessings. God wants to bless us with lives full of love, joy, peace, patience, kindness, goodness, gentleness, faithfulness, and self-control. If all of our lives were full of those things, I think it is safe to say we wouldn't want for anything else.

Yield Yourself to God's Will

We tend to think of asking as the part of prayer we like. We think of yielding as the part of prayer we don't like. This tells us something profound about what we believe about God: we don't really believe that God is good. We don't believe that yielding our life to Him will make our lives better. We don't really believe that He is a rewarder as it says in Hebrews 11:6, "But without faith it is impossible to please Him, for he who comes to God must believe that He is, and that He is a rewarder of those who diligently seek Him."

Joshua said, "But if serving the LORD seems undesirable to you, then choose for yourselves this day whom you will serve, whether the gods your ancestors served beyond the Euphrates, or the gods of the Amorites, in whose land you are living. But as for me and my household, we will serve the LORD" (Joshua 24:15, NIV). The key question is "Do you believe serving the Lord is desirable?" If you think it is desirable, you will gladly serve the Lord and His yoke really will become easy (Matthew 11:30). If you don't believe serving the Lord is desirable, no amount of commitment will keep you serving the Lord.

Prayer is not so much getting your will done in Heaven; it is getting God's will done in your life. It is not changing God's mind; it is God's means of changing you. People of prayer grow into people who exhibit love, joy, peace, and the rest of the fruit of the Spirit.

God wants to bless your socks off, but He will only pour His blessing on yielded people.

The message of the Bible is pretty simple, really: God is good. He has our best interest at heart. It is always in our best interest to live the Christian life over the long run. It may cost you in the short run, but in the long run, you will be glad you followed God. God is a rewarder. It is desirable to serve the Lord.

God's ways are good. Over and over in the Bible, we are commanded to be obedient "so that it may go well with you" (Deuteronomy 4:40; 12:25, 28; 19:13). We are indwelt with the person and power of the Holy Spirit because we cannot follow God on our own. One central truth of the Bible is simply this: God is good. It is always in our best interest to live the Christian life. It is always good for us to be obedient. It is always good for us to yield ourselves to God.

Expect God's Answer

Does God always answer prayers?
> Always.
> Do we always get what we ask for in prayer?
> No.
> God always does what is best in His infinite wisdom.

If the request is wrong, the answer will be "No." If the timing is wrong, the answer will be "Slow." If you are wrong, the answer will be "Grow." If the request is right, the timing is right, and you are right, the answer will be "Go!"

We tend to think that prayer is primarily about changing God to do what we want done. It is not. Prayer is primarily about changing us so that God can use us and pour His blessing on us. Richard Foster says, "Prayer is the central avenue God uses to transform us."[60]

We pray for God to heal, and He does heal. We pray for God to save, and He does save. We pray for God to provide, and He does provide. But while He is doing those things, He is transforming us. Prayer changes us more than it changes the things we pray about.

Repeat

You read it on the back of a shampoo bottle: lather, rinse, repeat. It applies to shampoo; it applies to prayer.

You don't just do it one day; you do it daily. You do it every day. Just as you wash yourself physically every day, you wash your soul every day. Just as you eat every day, you feed on the Word every day.

Steve Gaines advises that we make prayer the pattern of our lives.

YOU MUST PRAY CONTINUALLY

Jesus followed His teaching on the model prayer with this parable:

> *And He said to them, "Which of you shall have a friend, and go to him at midnight and say to him, 'Friend, lend me three loaves; for a friend of mine has come to me on his journey, and I have nothing to set before him'; and he will*

> *answer from within and say, 'Do not trouble me; the door is now shut, and my children are with me in bed; I cannot rise and give to you'? I say to you, though he will not rise and give to him because he is his friend, yet because of his persistence he will rise and give him as many as he needs. So I say to you, ask, and it will be given to you; seek, and you will find; knock, and it will be opened to you. For everyone who asks receives, and he who seeks finds, and to him who knocks it will be opened. (Luke 11:5–10)*

Here is the point: you must come to God in prayer continually. The tenses of the verb are consistently linear. It could be translated, "Keep on asking; keep on seeking; keep on knocking." You must bring your petitions persistently. You must pray about your burdens passionately. The Bible says we are to "pray without ceasing" (1 Thessalonians 5:17). The Bible says, "The effective, fervent prayer of a righteous man avails much" (James 5:16).

The story is told of a dad who told his son to move a rock. He gave him a crowbar and told him to go to work. He watched as the boy struggled and strained and sweated and grunted…to no avail.

He came and told his dad he couldn't move that rock. His dad asked some questions.

"Did you give it your all?"

"Yes."

"Did you use all your strength?"

"Yes."

"Did you use all your resources?"

"Yes."

"No you didn't; you didn't ask me to help."

Christian living is both active and passive. It is straining with all our might; it is asking the Father to help.

For too many Christians, Christian living is merely trying really hard to be good. This is not Christianity. This is the stuff of the Pharisees—the people on whom Jesus unleashed his most scathing rebuke.

Christian living does involve trying, but it is trying in the strength He provides (Colossians 1:29).

When we do that, all the riches and strength of heaven are made available to us.

YOU MUST PRAY CONFIDENTLY

"And whatever things you ask in prayer, believing, you will receive." (Matthew 21:22)

If a son asks for bread from any father among you, will he give him a stone? Or if he asks for a fish, will he give him a serpent instead of a fish? Or if he asks for an egg, will he offer him a scorpion? If you then, being evil, know how to give good gifts to your children, how much more will your heavenly Father give the Holy Spirit to those who ask Him! (Luke 11:11-13)

You have not because you ask not, or you ask amiss. (James 4:2-3)

God is more willing to answer than we are to ask.
Let me close this chapter with three prayers you can always pray:

- *Lord, save me.* God may not always grant your request of a miracle, but He will always grant your request for mercy. This is what Peter cried as he was walking on the water and looked at the waves and began to sink. Jesus reached down and lifted him up.
- *Lord, forgive me.* "If we confess our sins, He is faithful and just to forgive us our sins and to cleanse us from all unrighteousness" (1 John 1:9). Don't miss that little word "just." God would be unjust if He did not forgive your sins when you ask. The penalty for your sins was paid for on the cross. God would be unjust to charge that penalty against you as well.
- *Lord, use me.* Isaiah said, "Here am I! Send me" (Isaiah 6:8).

I close this chapter with one of my favorite quotes on prayer:

The great people of the earth today are the people who pray, [not] those who talk about prayer...but I mean those who take time and pray.
~S.D. Gordon

May we follow God in becoming people who take time to pray.

6

SHARE JESUS WITHOUT FEAR

Acts 1:8

The vast majority of Christians never share their faith with anyone. I read an article recently that told why. It listed the top ten reasons people don't share their faith. The #1 reason?

Fear.

You may feel this way. You may feel afraid to share your faith. If so, I'd like to invite you to take a fresh look at the last words of Jesus before He left planet earth.

> *But you shall receive power when the Holy Spirit has come upon you; and you shall be witnesses to Me in Jerusalem, and in all Judea and Samaria, and to the end of the earth." (Acts 1:8)*

We live in a world that desperately needs Jesus. Every time I watch the news I am impressed by what a mess our world is in. And here is what I know: Democrats don't have the answer. Republicans don't have the answer. The answer does not lie in politics. The answer does not lie in a better educational system. The problems on the world stage will not be solved with a stronger military or better diplomacy.

The world needs Jesus.

The problem in the world is a heart problem. We need changed hearts. We need hearts that are loving and kind and gracious and compassionate and caring and wise. Only Jesus can do that.

The world needs Jesus.

I believe in a literal Heaven and Hell. Eternity lasts a long time. Hell is a place of unspeakable torment. Heaven is available to anyone who will call upon the name of Jesus.

The world needs Jesus.

The vast majority of people who ever come to faith in Christ will do so because a friend or family member tells them about Jesus. Usually it starts with inviting them to church.

WHAT IS EVANGELISM?

The Greek word for evangelism is a combination of two underlying Greek words. Combined, they mean, "messengers of good news."

Let me emphasize this point. The message of the gospel is good news. The good news is that God loves us. He wants to help us and not harm us. He wants to bless and not curse. He wants to forgive and not punish. He sent Jesus to pay the penalty for our sins so that He could forgive. His righteousness would not allow Him to simply ignore our sins. He wants to give us an abundant, joyful, purposeful, peace-filled life.

I will make you a promise: most people do not see it this way. Ask them. Don't even try to convince them; just do some research. Pretend like you are a student working on a research project or a reporter working on a story.

Ask a few friends if they think following God would make their life better or worse. Ask a few friends if they think religion is good news or bad news. Ask a few friends if they believe God is crazy about them and wants to bless their socks off.

I am so glad I don't have to preach bad news each week. I am so glad I get to preach good news each week—the good news that there is a God in Heaven who is seated on the throne and has our best interest at heart. He has a plan for making this world a little more like Heaven and a little less like Hell. His plan is to change lives from the inside out.

This is the definition of evangelism that I was taught in seminary: "Evangelism is to so present Christ to men, that under the leadership, conviction, and inspiration of the Holy Spirit, they will see their need for a Savior and will receive Christ as Lord and Savior and serve Him through one of His churches."[61]

On the mission field they define success as "Evangelism that results in growing churches." Here is the point. The goal is not merely to present the gospel. The goal is not merely to get people to pray a prayer. The goal is to make disciples. The goal is to cooperate with God in creating disciples.

I see the way some people are involved in evangelism, and I cringe. It just seems weird to me. I don't think we help the cause of Christ by being weird. But we don't help the cause of Christ by being silent either.

I have known people who witness often, and often see people pray to receive Christ. Often people bow their head and pray the sinner's prayer. Then, they are never heard from again. They never come to church. They are never baptized. They never have an interest in follow up.

If you witness and this has been your experience, I have two words for you:

- *Good for you!* You are doing more than most. You are verbalizing your faith. You are being bold. You are trying. Good for you.
- *Be careful.* Be careful that you are not being weird for God. Ask a friend to go with you and give you honest feedback. Look carefully at the person to whom you witness. Be extra sensitive to their body language and non-verbal communication. Be careful that you do not overpower them with the strength of your personality. Keep in mind the goal is evangelism that results in discipleship.

Jesus spoke of "fruit that will last" (John 15:16). This is the goal of every believer—to have fruit that will last. Our goal is to so live that disciples are created. My dream for every believer is that there would be people in your life who would say, "She influenced me to follow Christ, and I am so glad she did."

Perhaps you are discouraged about evangelism. Perhaps you have a brother or a son or a neighbor or a friend that you have been praying for and witnessing to for years. You are so burdened for their eternal destiny. They don't appear to be coming around. Some days it seems like they are moving farther from God. You are tempted to give up. I wrote this chapter for you.

The first thing I want to say is this: don't give up. Keep praying. Keep being burdened. Keep witnessing. Don't give up. You are never a failure when you are obedient to share Jesus with the ones you know and love.

I talked to someone recently who had been praying for a brother for years. She got a little discouraged. She wanted to give up. It seemed like there was no progress. Then, he got saved.

When you are at the place where you are at the end of you rope and don't know what else to do, that is a good place to be. God can greatly use the person who is profoundly dependent on Him. God can't do much with a person who thinks he can witness in his own power.

Here is a key word for witnessing: be winsome. The Bible says we are to make the gospel attractive (Titus 2:10, NIV). The God's Word translation has it, "Then they will show the beauty of the teachings about God our Savior in everything they do." This verse categorically prohibits being weird for God.

How do we witness without being weird? More importantly, how do we engage in witnessing that results in making disciples?

UTILIZE THE POWER OF THE SPIRIT

Witnessing is not a debate where you try to convince people of the logic of the gospel. D.T. Niles said, "Witnessing is one beggar telling another beggar where to find bread."[62]

Effective witnessing is always done in the power of the Holy Spirit. It is always done with a profound awareness of the dependence on God. Acts 1:8 says, "You shall receive power when the Holy Spirit comes upon you."

The Greek word for power is the word we get from our word dynamite. The word suggests explosive, overwhelming power. Kittle says, "Words of this stem all have the basic sense of ability or capability. *Dýnamai* means 'to be able.'"[63] You are not able to witness on your own, or else God would not have sent the Holy Spirit. With the Holy Spirit, you are able.

Let's return to what we said about spiritual warfare. Do you remember the devil's power? It is the power to deceive. When he lies, he speaks his native language. He will try to deceive you at this point. He will try to convince you that you are not able.

As you read the paragraphs above you might have said to yourself, "I can't do that. I can't witness." That is not the voice of God in your head. The Bible says the Holy Spirit will give you power.

The Bible says of all believers, "Or do you not know that your body is the temple of the Holy Spirit who is in you, whom you have from God, and you are not your own? For you were bought at a price; therefore glorify God in your body and in your spirit, which are God's" (1 Corinthians 6:19–20).

All believers are the temple of God and are indwelt with the Holy Spirit, "For by one Spirit we were all baptized into one body—whether Jews or Greeks, whether slaves or free—and have all been made to drink into one Spirit" (1 Corinthians 12:13).

Anyone who does not have the Holy Spirit is not a Christian. "But you are not in the flesh but in the Spirit, if indeed the Spirit of God dwells in you. Now if anyone does not have the Spirit of Christ, he is not His" (Romans 8:9). Don't let anyone convince you that even though you are saved, you need the Holy Spirit. We don't need more of the Holy Spirit; the Holy Spirit needs more of us.

There is a distinction in Scripture between the indwelling of the Holy Spirit and the filling of the Holy Spirit. Every believer is indwelt with the Holy Spirit at conversion. We are also commanded to be continually filled with the Holy Spirit. "And do not be drunk with wine, in which is dissipation; but be filled with the Spirit" (Ephesians 5:18). The tense of the verb suggests ongoing, continual action. David Jeremiah says, "In essence, the text says, 'Be BEING filled with the Holy Spirit.' Continually give over control of your life to Him."[64]

The Holy Spirit didn't just come into your life to hang out. The Holy Spirit came into your life to empower you for evangelism. The Holy Spirit came into your life so He could work through you so you could tell others about Jesus. The main job of the Holy Spirit is to shine the light on Jesus. Acts 1:8 says that when the Holy Spirit comes upon us, we will be witnesses.

We get our word "martyr" from the Greek word translated *witness* because so many witnesses were martyred for their faith. Zodhiates says, "One who has information or knowledge of something, and hence, one who can give information, bring to light, or confirm something."[65]

The word has a legal connotation. It reminds us of someone who is called into a court of law to testify to what he has seen. The witness shares what he has experienced. The idea of witnessing is not so much that we recite a memorized presentation, as it is that we recall and communicate what we have experienced.

We are filled with the Spirit so we can witness, but there is more. Acts 4:31 says, "And when they had prayed, the place where they were assembled together was shaken; and they were all filled with the Holy Spirit, and they spoke the word of God with boldness."

Notice in this passage, as in Acts 1:8, there is a connection between filling of the Holy Spirit and being shaken. This is a reminder that our churches all need a good shaking with the Holy Spirit. We don't need a new program; we need to be shaken by the power of the Holy Spirit. It happened because they spent time in prayer. This is what our churches desperately need today—to spend time in prayer and be shaken by the power of the Holy Spirit.

Acts 4:31 goes on to say that they spoke the word of God with boldness. One Greek dictionary says this word means "outspokenness, frankness, plainness of speech, that conceals nothing and passes over nothing."[66] Notice there is nothing in this definition about being weird. Anyone can be a jerk. Only Holy Spirit-filled Christians can be bold.

THE HOLY SPIRIT CONVICTS THE LOST PERSON

You cannot convict. Only the Holy Spirit can convict.

Unless the Holy Spirit takes the Word of God spoken through the witness for God and convicts the heart of a sinner, there will be no conversion.

Jesus said of the Holy Spirit, "And when He has come, He will convict the world of sin, and of righteousness, and of judgment" (John 16:8).

No one can convict a sinner that he is a sinner except the Holy Spirit. Conviction suggests there is a sense of shame over their sin.[67] In one sense, everyone knows they are sinners. People commonly say, "No one is perfect." But it doesn't matter to them. Conviction is when it comes to matter.

The message of the gospel is that God takes sin very seriously. He hates it. It disgusts Him. It makes God sick. He can't stand it. He can't stand to be around it. He can't stand to be near it. Why? Because sins hurts the ones He loves.

He loves sinners. He is crazy about us. He longs for us. He loves us. He doesn't want anything to mess up our lives, so He can't stand sin.

What is God to do?

God solved this problem in the most amazing way in the person and work of Jesus. Jesus paid the penalty for our sins so we are free to come into the presence of the God who loves us. That is the gospel.

Until people understand the first half—how seriously God takes sin—they don't appreciate the need for the cross. Only the Holy Spirit can convict that sin is a big deal.

John 16:8 says that the Holy Spirit will convict us of our sin, His righteousness (and, by implication, the gap in between), and the judgment that is to come.

Do you ever wonder why there is so much evil in the world? Do you ever wonder why God doesn't do something about it? Here is one answer: He will.

Judgment is coming. Here are a few verses that speak of this:

- "For we must all appear before the judgment seat of Christ, that each one may receive the things done in the body, according to what he has done, whether good or bad." (2 Corinthians 5:10)
- "So then each of us shall give account of himself to God." (Romans 14:12)
- "And as it is appointed for men to die once, but after this the judgment." (Hebrews 9:27)
- "Then I saw a great white throne and Him who sat on it, from whose face the earth and the heaven fled away. And there was found no place for them. And I saw the dead, small and great, standing before God, and books were opened. And another book was opened, which is the Book of Life. And the dead were judged according to their works, by the things which were written in the books. The sea gave up the dead who were in it, and Death and Hades delivered up the dead who were in them. And they were judged, each one according to his works. Then Death and Hades were cast into the lake of fire. This is the second death. And anyone not found written in the Book of Life was cast into the lake of fire." (Revelation 20:11–15)

Until the Holy Spirit burns these words into a person's soul, they are just words. The Holy Spirit must convict us of our sin, His righteousness, and the judgment to come. When we witness, we are completely dependent on the Holy Spirit to convict.

This is true in every area of Christian living. We are completely dependent on the power of the Holy Spirit working in us. Christian living is not about trying really hard to be good. It does involve trying. But it is trying with a profound awareness that unless God empowers us, all our trying is in vain.

Jesus reserved His most scathing rebuke for those who tried really hard to be good—the Pharisees. Jesus taught us to be ever vigilant against the sin of the Pharisees—the sin of trying to live the Christian life in our own strength. Here are a couple of verses that clarify this:

- "To this end I also labor, striving according to His working which works in me mightily." (Colossians 1:29)
- "But by the grace of God I am what I am, and His grace toward me was not in vain; but I labored more abundantly than they all, yet not I, but the grace of God which was with me." (1 Corinthians 15:10)
- "Therefore, my beloved, as you have always obeyed, not as in my presence only, but now much more in my absence, work out your own salvation with fear and trembling; for it is God who works in you both to will and to do for His good pleasure." (Philippians 2:12-13)

This is true in witnessing, and it is true in every area of life. Christian living is lived trying hard while being profoundly aware that I can't live the Christian life without the power of the Holy Spirit working in my life.

THE HOLY SPIRIT CONVERTS THE LOST PERSON

It is the Holy Spirit that convicts, and it is the Holy Spirit that converts. "But when the kindness and the love of God our Savior toward man appeared, not by works of righteousness which we have done, but according to His mercy He saved us, through the washing of regeneration and renewing of the Holy Spirit" (Titus 3:4-5).

If you are tempted to believe, as some teach, that the Holy Spirit comes sometime after we are saved, look carefully at this verse. "He saved us through the… renewing of the Holy Spirit." You cannot be saved without being renewed by the Holy Spirit. You cannot be saved without receiving the Holy Spirit.

Occasionally someone will ask me if I believe in the second blessing. Yes, I believe in the second blessing… and the third blessing and fifth blessing and ten thousandth blessing. I believe in all the blessings of God. I also believe we are saved through the washing of regeneration AND the renewing of the Holy Spirit.

Only the Holy Spirit can convert. Only the Holy Spirit can change. Only the Holy Spirit can bring a dead soul to life. Only the Holy Spirit can save. The application for us to believe: we are completely dependent on the power of the Holy Spirit in sharing our faith. Unless He convicts of sin, there will be no salvation. Unless He converts the sinner, there will be no salvation.

The Holy Spirit is vitally important in witnessing. But the Holy Spirit does not draw attention to Himself. The Holy Spirit has been called "the shy member of the Trinity."[68] The Holy Spirit is crucial, but in witnessing, the spotlight is not on the Holy Spirit.

YOU MUST EMPHASIZE THE PERSON OF THE SON

When you witness, you need to do so with a constant awareness of and dependence on the Holy Spirit. But, don't talk about the Holy Spirit. Talk about Jesus. If you want to know what you say when you witness, here is the short answer: talk about Jesus.

Look again at Acts 1:8: "But you shall receive power when the Holy Spirit has come upon you; and you shall be witnesses to Me in Jerusalem, and in all Judea and Samaria, and to the end of the earth."

Notice the phrase "witnesses to Me."

Witnessing is not talking about yourself. It is talking about Jesus. There is a place in witnessing in telling your story. But the point of your story is to point to Jesus. Your story is not about you; it is about Jesus.

The emphasis of your testimony is not the drama of all the bad things you have done. The emphasis of your testimony is Jesus. Brag on Jesus!

Do you lack confidence in witnessing? Brag on Jesus. Don't know what to say? Brag on Jesus!

While writing this, I (Josh) had my first grandchild. I didn't have to take a class on how to tell someone about my grandchild. I didn't have to be reminded to post pictures on Facebook. You couldn't keep me from talking about my grandson. In fact, let me show you a picture of my one-day-old grandson:

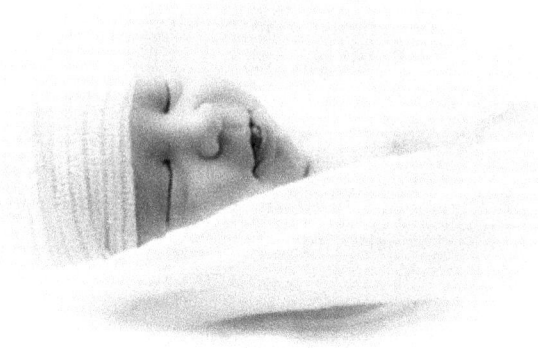

People who are thoroughly in love with Jesus talk about Him. I think in many cases we don't have a witnessing problem. We have a don't-love-Jesus-enough problem.

In Acts 8 we read the story of Phillip witnessing to the Ethiopian eunuch. The Ethiopian eunuch had been reading the Old Testament when Phillip approached him. Phillip started where the man was and took him to Jesus. "Then Philip opened his mouth, and beginning at this Scripture, preached Jesus to him" (Acts 8:35).

You don't win someone to Jesus by telling them what they need to quit doing. The Holy Spirit will convict them of what they ought not to do after they have been saved. Talk about what Phillip talked about: Jesus.

Notice also it says that Phillip opened his mouth. You can't be a witness unless you open your mouth. Occasionally I will have someone say to me that they witness with their life. Witnessing with your life is a good thing. Our lives should be a witness.

Francis of Assisi said, "Preach the gospel, and if necessary, use words." The truth is, words are necessary. The Bible says, "How shall they believe in Him of whom they have not heard?" (Romans 10:14). You cannot witness with a zipped lip. We ought to live lives that make the gospel attractive, but we still need to speak about Jesus.

One of the first people I led to Christ was Robbie Velasquez. He lived down the street from me in a share-croppers shack. I had just gotten saved and knew almost nothing about theology. I was just a young teenager. Robbie and I were hanging out one day, doing what teenagers do. I asked Robbie if he had ever been saved. I asked him if he knew Jesus. I didn't know any better than just to ask.

Robbie said, "No."

I told him about Jesus. I told him that Jesus died on the cross for him. I told him that Jesus was buried and rose from the grave. I told him that if he would surrender his life to Jesus, Jesus would save him. Robbie received Christ that day.

It is just that simple.

Paul said, "Moreover, brethren, I declare to you the gospel which I preached to you, which also you received and in which you stand, by which also you are saved, if you hold fast that word which I preached to you—unless you believed in vain. For I delivered to you first of all that which I also received: that Christ died for our sins according to the Scriptures, and that He was buried, and that He rose again the third day according to the Scriptures" (1 Corinthians 15:1–4).

That is the gospel. To add anything to it is to deny the power of the truth of God's Word. It is all about Jesus…

- Jesus died.
- Jesus was buried.
- Jesus rose again.
- Receive Jesus.

One more question: who are we to witness to? Acts 1:8 tells us.

WHO ARE WE TO WITNESS TO?

"But you shall receive power when the Holy Spirit has come upon you; and you shall be witnesses to Me in Jerusalem, and in all Judea and Samaria, and to the end of the earth." (Acts 1:8)

Witnessing starts at home. Jesus was near Jerusalem when He spoke these words. Jerusalem represents those people to whom you are closest. Jerusalem is your family. Jerusalem is your friends. Jerusalem is your co-workers and neighbors. This is where witnessing begins. Oscar Thompson said:

Now do not tell me about winning the world if you cannot love your neighbor. Do not tell me about winning the world if you do not take time to meet the needs of your own child or spouse.

You are to be a channel of love. Start in your "Jerusalem." Start in your home.[69]

Oscar Thompson uses this diagram to illustrate how the gospel moves through concentric circles, starting with the inner circles:

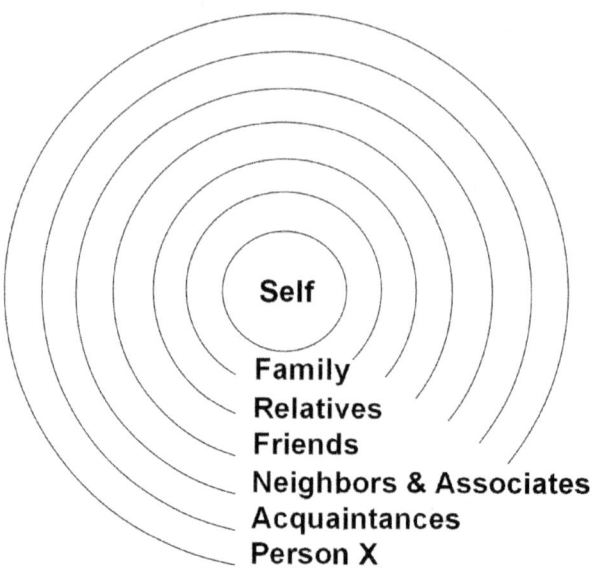

The gospel spreads best on existing lines of communication. The gospel spreads best to people you know best. Your best witnessing opportunities are to people you know best.

The Bible says, "Believe on the Lord Jesus Christ, and you will be saved, you and your household" (Acts 16:31). The Greek word for "household" is *oikos*. It means "people." You might say, "I am going to have my people over for dinner." The word is actually translated "people" in this verse in the NIV, "The days are coming, declares the Lord, when I will make a new covenant with the people of Israel and with the people of Judah" (Hebrews 8:8, NIV).

Your oikos is the people you spend Thanksgiving with. Your oikos is the people you watch fireworks with on the Fourth of July. Your oikos is the people whose names are in your cell phone. That is where witnessing should begin.

Witnessing should begin with our closest relationships, but it should not end there.

JUDEA, SAMARIA, AND THE ENDS OF THE EARTH

Judea was the area that surrounded Jerusalem—about the size of a county. Samaria was the county to the north. It was not only geographically farther away, but it was also culturally quite different.

The Jews hated the Samaritans as much as any skinhead hated a black person. To witness in Samaria is to not only cross a geographical barrier, it was also to bridge a cultural barrier.

A great example of this is David Wilkerson's ministry among the gangs of New York City. Here was a middle-class white preacher whom God called to minister to every race imaginable of poor, drug-dealing, violent, profane kids. New York City was not all that far geographically from where David Wilkerson lived; it was a million miles away culturally.

We need to be willing to talk to people who are not like us about Jesus. We start with our oikos, but we don't stop there. In order to reach the ends of the earth, we must cross over some cultural barriers.

Red and yellow, black and white,
They are precious in His sight.

Evangelism is concerned with the whole earth. We are not content until the whole world hears. Missions must be on our hearts because missions are on God's heart.

The world is getting smaller. For the first time in history you can get to any place on the planet in less than a day. World travel is affordable for the working class. We can send and receive live video in real time to any place on earth.

If you can't go, pray. If you can't go, give. Do what you can to get the gospel to the ends of the earth.

Christian living is about winning people to Jesus. Jesus taught that as we follow Him, He will make us into fishers of men (Matthew 4:19).

LEARNING TO WITNESS FROM JESUS

I'd like to close this chapter with six quick tips about witnessing taken from John 4. This is the story of Jesus witnessing to the woman at the well.

1. *Open with casual conversation.* Jesus started with asking for water. Start with emotionally intelligent, normal, casual conversation. Don't be weird. If they are into hunting, talk about hunting. If they are into football, talk about football.
2. *Overlook initial resistance.* The woman at the well attempted to divert the conversation with Jesus by talking about where was the best place to worship. The people you talk to might try to get you off track. They will bring up questions like, "Did Adam and Eve have belly buttons?" Who cares? Get the conversation back on Jesus. If they ask about the heathen in Africa, lead the conversation back to the heathen in the room.
3. *Appeal to their spiritual hunger.* There is a God-shaped vacuum in the heart of every human. People hunger for God, though they may not know what they hunger for.
4. *Deal with the seriousness of sin.* Don't overlook sin. The good news is only good news because we have all sinned and fallen short of the glory of God.
5. *Avoid religious arguments.*
6. *Focus their attention on Jesus.* Brag on Jesus. Tell them how much you love being a follower of Jesus. Jesus said, "And I, if I am lifted up from the earth, will draw all peoples to Myself" (John 12:32). Tell them that Jesus died for them and was buried and rose again on the third day. Tell them that if they call upon the name of the Lord, they will be saved.

You can't talk someone into being saved. If you could talk them into being saved, the devil could talk them out of being saved. Only the Holy Spirit can convict of sin and convince of truth. What we can do is to tell people how wonderful Jesus is. We can tell them how we love being followers of Christ. We can tell them that anyone who calls upon the Lord will be saved. We can start with those closest to us. We can't be satisfied until the whole world knows.

7

GROWING IN GIVING

2 Corinthians 9

Modern science has confirmed what the Bible has long taught: life is better for the generous. Generous people are happier, healthier, have better relationships, and live longer than greedy people.[70]

Everyone likes a generous person. We admire generous people. We build statues of generous people. Nobody ever built a statue of a greedy person. No one admires the greedy. No one wants to be greedy. Most of us are not all that surprised if we pick up a newspaper and read something like this:

> *Boston, MA (AHN) - A recent survey revealed that those who spend a reasonable amount of money on other people experience greater elation than those who buy things for themselves. Scientists from the Harvard Business School gathered 632 Americans and questioned them about their income, their spending habits, and their level of happiness.*
>
> *Separately, the experts gathered 16 professionals up for a bonus between $3,000 and $8,000, and asked them similar questions six to eight weeks before and after the bonus.*

> *For the first experiment, results showed that the respondents' income level was a non-factor to the level of happiness, which was higher for those who spent money for others compared to those who merely spent for themselves. The second experiment showed that the increase in the employees' level of happiness was not affected by the size of the bonus. However, it appeared to rise in relation to the amount of money the employees spent on others or had given to charity, according to the Guardian.*
>
> *"Most people would think that if you make more money you are going to be a lot happier," said Harvard's Professor Michael Norton. "Our results, and a lot of other people's results, show that making more money makes you a little bit happier but doesn't really have a huge impact on you. Our studies suggest maybe that little changes in how you spend it make a difference."*
>
> *The Telegraph reported that a follow-up experiment wherein the experts gave respondents either $5 or $20 to be spent the way they see fit revealed that those who spend the money on others reported being happier compared to those who spent it on themselves.*[71]

Getting and keeping money doesn't make us any happier. Yet, we all have a tendency to grab and to keep. We enjoy watching *Hoarders* because there is a little hoarder in all of us. We may not be extreme hoarders as we see on TV, but all of us have a tendency to want to grab and keep.

Can I confess my sin to you? I have a tendency to want to grab and keep. I am making progress, but I am not where I want to be yet. Perhaps you feel the same way. How can we become the generous people God wants us to be and at least a part of us wants to be? The Bible offers answers.

GENEROSITY STARTS WITH UNDERSTANDING OWNERSHIP

Understanding giving starts with understanding ownership. It starts with understanding that we are stewards and not owners.

What is stewardship? I like Ron Blue's definition:

The use of God-given resources for the accomplishment of God-given goals.[72]

A steward is someone who manages things that don't belong to him. That is you and me. Nothing you own belongs to you. It is God's. You merely manage what belongs to God.

Your house does not belong to you. Your car does not belong to you. Your children do not belong to you. Your bank account does not belong to you. You don't even belong to you. It all belongs to God.

"The earth is the LORD's, and all its fullness, the world and those who dwell therein" (Psalm 24:1). God doesn't just own the cattle on a thousand hills (Psalm 50:10). He owns the hills!

I have a son named Jack. We have a room in our house we call "Jack's room." We have clothes we call "Jack's clothes." We have toys we call "Jack's toys." But, the truth is, Jack doesn't have a room. He doesn't have clothes, and he doesn't have toys. They all belong to me. He is just a steward of those things—and not always a very good steward!

Our Heavenly Father does the same thing. He lets us use things in the same way that I let Jack use things. But everything we have belongs to God. "As each one has received a gift, minister it to one another, as good stewards of the manifold grace of God" (1 Peter 4:10). Technically, this verse is talking about spiritual gifts, but the principle applies to all things. We are to use the things God has given us as good stewards.

The Bible contains a long list of things given to us by God…

- He gives us Sabbath and safety.
- He gives us showers and security.
- He gives us silence and sustenance.
- He gives us sleep and strength.
- He gives us smarts and salvation.

He gives all these things, not to possess as our own, but to manage as stewards.

You have been blessed to be a blessing. You have received that you might return. You have gotten so that you might give. One of the greatest and most fulfilling things you will ever do is to live out this calling.

BRAGGING ON THE CORINTHIANS

If you are a student of the Bible, you know that the church in Corinth was not the greatest church that Paul started. They had multiple problems. But there is one area where Paul brags that the Corinthians had excelled:

> *Now concerning the ministering to the saints, it is superfluous for me to write to you; for I know your willingness, about which I boast of you to the Macedonians, that Achaia was ready a year ago; and your zeal has stirred up the majority. (2 Corinthians 9:1-2)*

Paul brags on this church that it is a giving church. It has the reputation of being a generous church. This church was so generous that its example inspired others to give.

Did you know that generosity is contagious? That is what Paul says here—that the Corinthians' generosity had infected the church at Achaia. Again, science has confirmed what the Bible reveals that generosity is contagious:

> *One person's initial generosity can spark a chain reaction of benevolence, according to the latest study from prolific social contagion researchers James Fowler and Nicholas Christakis.*
>
> *To test their theory about the potential spread of cooperation and generosity, Fowler and Christakis recruited volunteers who didn't know one another, and ensured that every individual interacted with each other participant only once to rule out the possibility that generosity might be the result of increasing familiarity.*
>
> *Subjects participated in games in which they had the opportunity to foster cooperation by contributing money to others (in what the researchers referred to as a "public-goods game"). They found that, compared with those who hadn't benefited from others' generosity, study participants who received money in an earlier game were more likely to give money in a later game. Ultimately, the initial person's contribution was multiplied up to three times—a result in keeping with earlier findings on social contagion, suggesting*

GROWING IN GIVING

that this sort of ripple effect continues for three degrees of separation.

Though it may be encouraging to learn that altruism can be passed on through social networks— particularly in light of recent tragedies in Haiti and Chile that left so many people in need of help and kindness—the study also found that selfish, uncooperative behavior tended to spread through groups.[73]

One of the most influential qualities you can develop is the quality of generosity. Everyone loves a generous person. Most of us want to be generous people, but we struggle against our own greed.

Generosity is not just about money. It is an attitude. It is a way of life. Greed is not just about money. It is a me-first mindset. God wants to save us from the me-first mindset that plagues us all. Your generosity is not only a sign of your own spiritual growth, it is also an inspiration to everyone in your world. When they see your generosity, they will be inspired to be more generous themselves.

Generosity is not about a dollar amount. It is not about the number of dollars that are raised; it about the level of faith that is revealed. In Mark 12:41 and the following verses, we read the story of Jesus observing a woman giving two mites—a quarter of a cent. Jesus said of her, "Assuredly, I say to you that this poor widow has put in more than all those who have given to the treasury" (Mark 12:43).

Paul brags on the Corinthians' generosity, but he does one more thing—he prods them to follow through:

Yet I have sent the brethren, lest our boasting of you should be in vain in this respect, that, as I said, you may be ready; lest if some Macedonians come with me and find you unprepared, we (not to mention you!) should be ashamed of this confident boasting. Therefore I thought it necessary to exhort the brethren to go to you ahead of time, and prepare your generous gift beforehand, which you had previously promised, that it may be ready as a matter of generosity and not as a grudging obligation. (2 Corinthians 9:3-5)

Paul knew what we know. People get busy. People forget. People get behind on their giving. They skip a month. When people skip a month on their giving, they generally don't do what they do with their light bill. If you miss a light bill, they likely won't turn off your electricity. But, when you get your next bill, you will notice it is twice as big as the bill last month. You don't just have to pay this month; you need to pay last month as well. This is what happens when you get behind.

Happily, in the day in which we live, we never have to worry about this if we don't want to. I want to offer a suggestion that will flat out take the stew out of stewardship. If you feel guilty about getting behind and not being as generous as you want, I have an idea that will absolutely set you free.

Make giving automatic.

Set it up with your bank so that every time you get paid, a gift goes to your church and/or anyone else. You can do this online, or, if you are technologically challenged, go in to your bank and ask your banker if they can set up an automatic payment for you. You set it and forget it. No fuss; no muss. You will never have to feel guilty about not giving as much as you want again.

It might appear that Paul is trying to make people feel guilty. I don't think so. Paul was simply reminding them of what they had promised to do. He was getting them in touch with their own desire to be generous.

Paul knew what every pastor knows: people don't give out of guilt. They might give a time or two out of guilt, but they won't give for long. No one becomes a generous, graceful, cheerful giver because of guilt. We don't give out of guilt; we give in response to grace.

How can we become a generous, graceful, cheerful giver? Four things.

YOU MUST LEARN TO GIVE ABUNDANTLY

There are some people who want to give as little as they possibly can. Adrian Rogers used to say, "When it comes to giving, some people will stop at nothing."

Not me. I don't want to give as little as I can; I want to give as much as I can. I want to live abundantly, and I want to give abundantly. Paul offers a farming illustration:

> *But this I say: He who sows sparingly will also reap sparingly, and he who sows bountifully will also reap bountifully. (2 Corinthians 9:6)*

If you give little, you will reap little. If you give generously, you will reap generously. Perhaps Paul was thinking of this Proverb when he wrote:

> *There is one who scatters, yet*
> *increases more;*
> *And there is one who withholds*
> *more than is right,*
> *But it leads to poverty.*
> *The generous soul will be made rich,*
> *And he who waters will also be*
> *watered himself.*
> *(Proverbs 11:24–25)*

Some people, even in the church world, fundamentally misunderstand stewardship. They think being a good steward is being a tight-wad. I have had the experience (as most preachers have) of spending a good part of a week preparing to deliver a sermon, only to receive an honorarium that would barely cover lunch. Could you work for two or three days only to receive enough to cover one meal?

The people who made this decision probably thought they were being good stewards. In their minds, being a good steward meant hanging on to their money. That is not good stewardship; that is greediness. The Bible says we are to give abundantly. God's call for all of us is to have generous hearts.

Some people just want to. . .

Get all you can;
Can all you get;
Sit on the can and
Poison the rest.

Jesus is our example. He didn't just barely give enough; He gave His all. How do we give like Jesus gave?

Give First

The Old Testament called the tithe the "first fruits." It was called the first fruits because the people were to give first. They didn't have money as we do today, so they would give part of their harvest—the first part of their harvest. They would give the first lamb born of the flock.

They did not do what people sometimes do today—pay anybody and everybody first before they do their giving. I will make a promise to you: you will never be a generous giver if you give to God last. You will never be a generous giver if you give to God your leftovers.

Malachi 3:10 speaks of the tithes and the offerings. "Tithe" simply means "tenth." Offerings are what we give above the tithe.

The tithe is the starting point. Offerings are given above the tithe. If you tithe, I applaud your generosity. Still, I would invite you to see that in the Bible, the tithe is the starting point, not the finish line of giving. It is the floor, not the ceiling.

Here's what we do and what we recommend for you to do: when you get paid, make the first check your giving check. (Better to make an automatic draft as discussed above.)

Many people do the opposite. They get paid, and they start paying their bills. They pay their electric bill, their mortgage, their cell phone bill, the Jet Ski payment, and so on. If they have anything left, they give to God. This is not the biblical pattern.

Give Our Best

The situation in Malachi's time addressed this very issue. The people were bringing sickly lambs and moldy grain. Malachi challenged them to give their best to God. They were bringing things they wouldn't or couldn't use, giving them to God, and acting like they had done something heroic.

We preachers see this all the time. Someone has a piano that won't stay in tune so they give it to the church. They have an old couch with holes in it, and they give it to the church. All the while, they pat themselves on the back for their generosity. This is not biblical giving. God calls for us to give first, and He calls for us to give our best.

The same is true in giving our service to God. We've all seen singers who stepped to the microphone in church and clearly have not practiced. You may have attended a Bible Study where the teacher had clearly not prepared. The Bible says to give God your best.

Years ago the Butterball Company set up a hotline to help people with their turkey preparation. They received a call from a lady who said, "I have a turkey that has been in my deep freeze for thirteen years. Is it still safe to eat?"

The operator explained that if it had been kept below zero the entire time, it probably would be safe, although it might not be as tasty as if it were fresh. Because of taste, not safety, the operator recommended she throw it away and get a new one.

"That's what we thought; we will just give it to the church."

The Lord deserves our best, not our leftovers. He deserves excellence, not hand-me-downs. As the old hymn said it, "Give of your best to the Master."

I have been in churches where people lived in million-dollar homes, drove fifty-thousand-dollar cars, and traveled the world on sightseeing adventures. Yet, when you look at the building that they worshiped in, it is in shambles. This ought not to be.

The prophet Haggai asked in his day, "Is it time for you yourselves to dwell in your paneled houses, and the temple to lie in ruins?" (Haggai 1:4). That is a disgrace to grace! Give of your best to the Master.

Do you know why "The generous soul will be made rich" (Proverbs 11:25)? You have proven that God can trust you with what He's already given to you, so He keeps pouring it on so you can keep pouring out.

You can't out give God. He fills up your thimble; you pour it out; He fills it up. He fills up that five-gallon bucket; you pour it out; He fills it up. He fills that that swimming-pool-sized tank; you pour it out; He fills it up. You can't out give God.

YOU MUST LOVE TO GIVE CHEERFULLY

I have been in black congregations where they demonstrated this visibly. When the offering time came, everyone stood up for a standing ovation before the giving of the offering. I think every church should adopt this practice.

The Bible says:

So let each one give as he purposes in his heart, not grudgingly or of necessity; for God loves a cheerful giver. (2 Corinthians 9:7)

Notice, by the way, it says "purposed," not "prodded." "Not grudgingly" suggests that we give out of grace, not out of guilt.

God says that if you don't want to give, He doesn't want to receive. God doesn't need your money. As we saw earlier, it's not your money. It's God's money. If He wants to get it back, He can. He owns it all anyway. He doesn't need your charity.

What God does want is for you to get in on the blessing of giving. He wants you to know what science has just now learned—that generous people are happy people.

What does it mean to give grudgingly? I heard the story of one man who grudgingly made his alimony payments. He got down to the final payment, took his shirt off, and wrote the check on the back of the shirt. The amount was $182. The bank cashed it. That is giving grudgingly. God says if you give with that kind of attitude, keep your money. He doesn't need your money. He doesn't want your money. He wants you to know the blessing of becoming a generous soul.

The word translated "cheerfully" in this passage is the word *hilarós*. We get our word hilarious from this word. In other words, we are supposed to get giddy when the offering plate is passed.

YOU MUST LOOK TO GIVE EXPECTANTLY

We ought to give with joyful expectation that God will bless. We ought to expect God to bless the giver, and we ought to expect God to bless the gift.

The Bible says, "And my God shall supply all your needs according to His riches in glory by Christ Jesus" (Philippians 4:19). God promises to supply your needs; He will supply a number of your wants as well.

Let me be clear: this is not health and wealth gospel. I am not saying that because you tithe you will drive a BMW or live in a mansion. I am saying that God is generous. God is gracious. God will bless.

If you tithe and learn to give abundantly, God will supply all of your needs—not your greed, but your needs. The person who learns to tithe and give abundantly will be better off financially than the person who doesn't.

You may feel like you cannot afford to tithe. You have been deceived by the devil. You can't afford not to tithe. You can't afford to be outside the flow of God's blessing. You cannot rob God of His tithe and get away with it. In Haggai chapter 1, the Bible talks about the idea that if you rob from God, He will poke holes in your purse.

God not only blesses the giver, but He blesses the gift. This means you are to pray over your gift. Ask God to bless your gift. You are to look down the road in eager anticipation to see what God is going to do with your gift.

Now may He who supplies seed to the sower, and bread for food, supply and multiply the seed you have sown and increase the fruits of your righteousness, while you are enriched in everything for all liberality, which causes thanksgiving through us to God. For the administration of this service not only supplies the needs of the saints, but also is abounding through many thanksgivings to God, while, through the proof of this ministry, they glorify God for the obedience of your confession to the gospel of Christ, and for your liberal sharing with them and all men, and by their prayer for you, who long for you because of the exceeding grace of God in you. (2 Corinthians 9:10–14)

Ministry costs money. It costs money to put on outreach events. It costs money to pay the salaries of missionaries. It costs money to have effective children's and student ministries. It costs money to pay for the church buildings where we worship. It costs money to pay the light bill. We are to pray that God will richly bless the money we give to His kingdom.

YOU MUST LEARN TO GIVE THANKFULLY

Second Corinthians 9:15 is one of my favorite verses in all the Bible:

Thanks be to God for His indescribable gift! (2 Corinthians 9:15)

God's indescribable gift inspires us to be generous givers. God gave His first. God gave His best. God's indescribable gift ought to motivate us to be abundant, generous, expectant givers.

Gustave M. Hauser and Rita E. Hauser gave $13 million to the Harvard Law School. At the time, it was the largest single gift in the history of the law school. What would motivate such a gift?

Gratitude.

Gustave and Rita met at Harvard in 1955. They married the day after final exams. They went on to become highly successful in business.

Rita Hauser has practiced law as a senior partner of the firm Stroock & Stroock & Lavan. She is now counsel to the firm and participates in numerous philanthropic endeavors as president of the Hauser Foundation, chair of the International Peace Academy, and co-chair of the RAND Greater Middle East Studies Center.

Gustave Hauser was the chair and CEO of Hauser Communications. He was one of the pioneers of the modern cable television industry and had a hand in such breakthrough endeavors as Music Television (MTV) and Nickelodeon, a children's network.[74]

The Hausers had such deep gratitude to Harvard for its role in preparing them for their successful careers and for its role in being a matchmaker for them that their hearts overflowed in generosity. He said, "The school had a unique role in bringing us together."[75]

When we understand how profoundly God has given to us, we just naturally want to give. When we appreciate how much God has done for us, our hearts overflow with desire to give to others.

God gave His indescribable gift in the person of Jesus. Our greatest joy is in giving back of our time, our talents, our tithe, and our gifts to God.

8

FIRST PLACE

Matthew 6:33

The Lord Jesus wants to move into your life and transform it. The Lord Jesus wants to move into your life and make your life abundant, rich, and full. The Lord Jesus wants to give you a life marked by the fruit of the Spirit: love, joy, peace, longsuffering, kindness, goodness, faithfulness, gentleness, and self-control (Galatians 5:22, 23).

However, when the Lord Jesus moves into your life, He is still Lord. He will not move into your life as vice president. If the world's greatest violinist joined your orchestra, he would not join to play second fiddle. When Jesus moves in, He moves in as who He is: Lord.

Many seem to want God to be a part of their life but not to be their life. Many want to add Jesus as an accessory. They like the bumper sticker that says, "God is my co-pilot." God is not ever anyone's co-pilot. He is either the Pilot, or He will step out of the way and let you pilot your life.

To paraphrase C.S. Lewis, "There are two kinds of people in this world: those who say, 'Thy will done,' and those to whom God will say, 'thy will be done.'" He is Lord of all or not Lord at all.

Of course, no one lives this perfectly. The problem with a living sacrifice (Romans 12:1) is that it keeps crawling off the altar.

Surrendering to Christ as Lord is done the first time in salvation. Surrendering to Christ as Lord becomes the daily prayer of a disciple in his quiet time. Surrendering to Christ as Lord becomes as constant as breathing for the growing disciple.

Jesus said, "Seek first the kingdom of God and His righteousness, and all these things shall be added to you" (Matthew 6:33).

Jesus is saying two things:

1. Put first things first.
2. He's first.

Notice it is a conditional promise. You can't have the provision, "all these things will be added to you" without meeting the condition, "seek first the kingdom."

PUT FIRST THINGS FIRST

Seek means to actively pursue. It means to go intently after. It is often translated "look for" and describes those times when you lose something. Suppose you realized just now that your wallet was lost. Could you relax? Could you go on reading this book?

The word is used in this sense in the story of the woman and the lost coin, "Or what woman, having ten silver coins, if she loses one coin, does not light a lamp, sweep the house, and search carefully until she finds it?" (Luke 15:8).

When you lose something, you get really focused about trying to find it. That focus is what Jesus had in mind when He spoke of seeking first the kingdom. Just as when you lose something and you can't think of anything else until you find it, we are to have that kind of focus on seeking first the kingdom.

The word *seek* is in the present tense, which is a linear tense in the Greek. It suggests we are to continually seek first the kingdom. It is not something that happens once. It is our life-long vocation.

START WITH THE KING

Seeking first the kingdom starts with seeking first the King of the Kingdom. You can't have a kingdom without a King.

The Christian life is not merely about accepting Christ as Savior. It is also about the daily practice of seeking a relationship with Christ.

The Lord is not someone you passively accept. He is someone you actively seek. Augustine said that, unless you value Christ above all, you don't value Him at all.

You are as close to God as you want to be. Everyone who wants to seek Him finds Him. Everyone who wants to draw near to God is near to God. Everyone who wants to have the John 10:10 abundant Christian life has it.

Adrian Rogers used to say, "God doesn't have favorites, but He does have intimates." The Bible says, "You will seek Me and find Me, when you search for Me with all your heart" (Jeremiah 29:13). "Draw near to God and He will draw near to you" (James 4:8).

It isn't enough to seek the Lord. You must seek *first* the kingdom. We don't just search for Him. We search for Him *with all our heart*. The consistent command of the Bible is this: put God first. It is the first of the Ten Commandments.

Jesus wants the first moments of every day. He wants the first day of every week. He wants the first dollar of every paycheck.

WHAT IS THE KINGDOM OF GOD?

The kingdom of God is the place where God rules and reigns. It is the realm where Jesus is recognized as King.

Everyone has a kingdom. Your kingdom is where you get your way. It is where what you say goes. Dallas Willard said:

> *The kingdom of God is the range of God's effective will, where what God wants done is done. Earth and its immediate surroundings seem to be the only place in creation where God permits his will to not be done. Therefore we pray, "Thy kingdom come, Thy will be done in earth, as it is in heaven" (Matthew 6:10, KJV) and hope for the time when that kingdom will be completely fulfilled even here on earth, where, in fact, it is already present (see Luke 17:21) and available to those who seek it with all their heart (see Matthew 6:33; 11:12; Luke 16:16). For those who seek it, it is true even now that all things work together for their good and that nothing can cut them off from God's inseparable love and effective care (see Romans 8:28, 35–39).*[76]

In the verse cited above, Jesus said, "The kingdom of God is within you" (Luke 17:21). When Jesus reigns as Lord in our hearts, the kingdom of God is present, right here, right now. Jesus taught us to pray, "Your kingdom come. Your will be done on earth as it is in heaven" (Matthew 6:10).

What is it like in God's kingdom? What is it like when we surrender to Him as Lord? Paul described it this way, "For the kingdom of God is not eating and drinking, but righteousness and peace and joy in the Holy Spirit" (Romans 14:17). Life in the kingdom is a life marked by the fruit of the Spirit: love, joy, peace…

WHAT DOES IT MEAN TO SEEK FIRST THE KINGDOM OF GOD?

To seek first the kingdom means to seek God's glory. "Therefore, whether you eat or drink, or whatever you do, do all to the glory of God" (1 Corinthians 10:31). To seek first the kingdom is to become obsessed about God being glorified. We want God to be respected and acknowledged and looked up to. We want Him to be treated as He is worthy of being treated. It bothers you to hear His Name disrespected.

To seek first the kingdom is to seek God's guidance. A loyal subject will always do what the King wants him to do. There is no higher calling in life than following the King in loyal obedience. There is no greater joy in life than following the King in obedience. If you want to make the rest of your life the best of your life, seek first the guidance of the King. We would do well to start every day and say with the Apostle Paul, "What shall I do, Lord?" (Acts 22:10).

Seeking first the kingdom means seeking God's governance. A loyal subject desires to be controlled by the King. Why would you desire to be controlled by the King? Because God is good. Because following Him is good. Because it is always in our best interest to live the Christian life. It is always good for us to follow God. In the long run, it always benefits us to be obedient to God.

Life in the flesh is essentially this: I don't want anyone telling me what to do. I don't like my boss telling me what to do. I don't like my wife telling me what to do. I don't want my preacher to tell me what to do. I don't want my God to tell me what to do. In fact, I will tell Him what to do: bless me, and bless me indeed.

This is not biblical Christianity, and it never works. Jesus comes into our lives as Lord, or He does not come in at all.

This is what life has taught me: the great joy in life comes from being controlled by the right Master. There is no greater joy than living under the Lordship of Christ. Life at its best is lived under the complete control of God. It would be better to die in the will of God than to live outside of the will of God.

AND HIS RIGHTEOUSNESS...

Jesus goes on to say, "Seek first the kingdom of God *and His righteousness.*" The sense of it is that His righteousness would be fleshed out in our lives. We are to seek a life of living righteously. We are to seek God's control over us and God's character inside of us. The Kingdom of God is not just inwardly experienced; it is outwardly expressed. If God is ruling over you, His righteousness will be within you.

You can always tell a person's faith by their fruit. You can always see their character by their conduct. We will never make a difference in this world until the world can see a difference in our lives.

Gandhi said, "I like your Christ; I do not like your Christians. Your Christians are so unlike your Christ."[77] The mark of a real Christian is that He makes it easier for others to believe in God.

Seeking first the righteousness of God means we want to be righteous. We do what we really want to do. Sometimes people say things to me like...

- Pastor, I really want to be a person of prayer.
- Pastor, I really want to be generous giver.
- Pastor, I really want to be a soul-winner.

I appreciate the sentiment. But, in the long run, you do what you really want to do. You pray as much as you really want to pray. You give as much as you really want to give. You serve as much as you really want to serve. You are about as close to God as you really want to be. No one who really wants to be close to God is far from God.

Jesus said, "Blessed are those who hunger and thirst for righteousness, for they shall be filled" (Matthew 5:6). "Hunger and thirst" suggest a deep desire.

Christianity is the exact opposite of the teachings of Buddha. In Buddhism, desire is the problem. Suffering is seen as desiring things we can't get. The solution, then, is to kill desire.

Christianity is about stirring up good desire. It is about becoming a person who hungers and thirsts for righteousness. John Eldridge speaks eloquently about this:

> *"We abandon the most important journey of our lives when we abandon desire. We leave our hearts by the side of the road and head off in the direction of fitting in, getting by, being productive, what have you. Whatever we might gain—money, position, the approval of others, or just absence of the discontent itself–it's not worth it. "What good will it be for a man if he gains the whole world, yet forfeits his soul?" (Matthew 16:26, NIV).*
>
> *The greatest enemy of holiness is not passion; it is apathy.*
>
> *Killing desire may look like sanctification, but it's really godlessness. Literally, our way of handling life without God.*
>
> *Without a deep and burning desire of our own, we will be ruled by the desires of others.*[78]

One of the great writers on prayer is E.M. Bounds. He too spoke of the importance of hungering and thirsting after righteousness—the importance of desire:

> *Desire gives fervor to prayer. The soul cannot be listless when some great desire fixes and inflames it . . . Strong desires make strong prayers . . . The neglect of prayer is the fearful token of dead spiritual desires . . . There can be no true praying without desire.*[79]

We must desire to live righteously as much as a hungry man wants to eat and a thirsty man wants to drink.

HIS RIGHTEOUSNESS

Christianity is not about trying really hard to be good. We make a mess of Christianity when we pursue our own righteousness rather than the righteousness of God. God is not interested in what you can do for Him; He is interested in what He can do through you.

It is a great day in the life of the average believer when he or she learns the difference between self-righteousness and Savior-righteousness. Paul said, "…and be found in Him, not having my own righteousness, which is from the law, but that which is through faith in Christ, the righteousness which is from God by faith" (Philippians 3:9).

The theological term for this is *imputed* righteousness. Dictonary.com defines imputed as "to attribute to a person or persons vicariously."⁸⁰ The key verse is "For He made Him who knew no sin to be sin for us, that we might become the righteousness of God in Him" (2 Corinthians 5:21). Righteousness must be imputed before it can be imparted. You have to receive righteousness before you can live righteously. God has to give it before you can live it.

On your best day, the best things you do are like filthy rags in the sight of a holy God (Isaiah 64:6). Godly Christians are profoundly aware of this. They know they cannot live the Christian life by simply trying really hard to be good.

But Christian living is not altogether passive, either. It is both active and passive. It is trying like it all depended on you and trusting like it all depended on God. It is witnessing like an Arminian and sleeping like a Calvinist. The Bible says, "To this end I also labor, striving according to His working which works in me mightily" (Colossians 1:29). The NIV translates it, "To this end I strenuously contend with all the energy Christ so powerfully works in me" (Colossians 1:29, NIV).

THE PROMISE

"...and all these things will be added to you."

What things?

All the things you tend to worry about.

In verse 19 and following, Jesus talks about money. Are you ever tempted to worry about money? Jesus said it will be added unto you as you seek first the kingdom and His righteousness.

> *"Do not lay up for yourselves treasures on earth, where moth and rust destroy and where thieves break in and steal; but lay up for yourselves treasures in heaven, where neither moth nor rust destroys and where thieves do not break in and steal. For where your treasure is, there your heart will be also." (Matthew 6:19–21)*

You can't take it with you, but you can send it ahead of you. I have done a lot of funerals in my life. Not one time have I seen a U-Haul being pulled behind a hearse. We come in naked and bankrupt, and we go out naked and bankrupt.

Verse 25 says not to worry about food and clothes:

> *"Therefore I say to you, do not worry about your life, what you will eat or what you will drink; nor about your body, what you will put on. Is not life more than food and the body more than clothing?" (Matthew 6:25)*

The Lord knows that you need these things:

> *"For after all these things the Gentiles seek. For your heavenly Father knows that you need all these things." (Matthew 6:32)*

The Lord knows that you need them. If you will seek first the kingdom of God and His righteousness, He will take care of all these things.

"All these things" speaks of your need. Paul said, "And my God shall supply all your need according to His riches in glory by Christ Jesus" (Philippians 4:19). Note the word: "need." The promise is that God will supply all of your need, not all of your greed. You may not have everything you want, but you will have everything you need and a lot of the things you want.

If you don't have something that you want, it is because God knows you don't need it right now. It is our job to serve Him; it is His job to supply us. Many have that backwards. They think it is God's job to serve us and our job to supply us.

I heard the story of a young missionary going overseas before the days of air travel. As he was walking up the gangplank, a rich friend approached him with an envelope. He looked him in the eye and said, "If you ever get to the end of your rope and don't know where else to turn, open this envelope."

Thirty years later, the missionary returned. His rich friend greeted him. "Still got that envelope?"

The missionary pulled it out of his pocket.

"Are you telling me that you didn't get to the end of your rope—not one time in thirty years?"

"Never, not one time, did I come to the place where I didn't know what else to do or where to turn, because He was with me."

If you want to make the rest of your life the best of your life, put Christ first. He will resource those who reverence Him.

ENDNOTES

1. http://homeguides.sfgate.com/root-system-oak- trees-48319.html

2. http://www.blackchristiannews.com/news/2013/10/80-of- americans-identify-as-christians-but-far-fewer-are-church- members-what-should-the-church-do-to.html

3. Gerhard Kittel, Gerhard Friedrich, and Geoffrey William Bromiley, *Theological Dictionary of the New Testament* (Grand Rapids, MI: W.B. Eerdmans, 1985), 1132.

4. Tony Evans, *Totally Saved*. Moody Press: Chicago, 2002, pg. 17)

5. https://www.youtube.com/watch?v=uKCEWxVsOEo

6. http://www.touchjesussongs.net/lyricspage15.html

7. John Stott, *The Cross of Christ* (Downers Grove: Inter Varsity Press, 1986), 160.

8. Bruce, F. F. *Romans: An Introduction and Commentary. Vol. 6. Tyndale New Testament Commentaries*. Downers Grove, IL: InterVarsity Press, 1985.

9. Hershel H. Hobbs, *New Men in Christ: Studies in Ephesians*, (Waco: Word Books, 1974) pg. 15.

10. http://listverse.com/2010/07/17/10-incredibly-painful-rites- of-initiation/

11. Millard J. Erickson, *Introducing Christian Doctrine, 2nd ed.* (Grand Rapids, MI: Baker Academic, 2001), 358.

12. Rick Warren, *The Purpose Driven Church: Growth Without Compromising Your Message and Mission* (Grand Rapids, MI: Zondervan, 2007).

13. *Baptist Faith and Message* http://www.sbc.net/bfm2000/ bfm2000.asp

14. Herbert, Wray (2010-09-14). *On Second Thought: Outsmarting Your Mind's Hard-Wired Habits* (p. 30). Crown Publishing Group. Kindle Edition.

15. Lyubomirsky, Sonja (2007-12-27). *The How of Happiness: A New Approach to Getting the Life You Want* (pp. 148-149). Penguin Group. Kindle Edition.

16. Josh Hunt, *Christian Hospitality*, 2007.

17. Achor, Shawn (2010-09-14). *The Happiness Advantage: The Seven Principles of Positive Psychology That Fuel Success and Performance at Work* (p. 176). Crown Publishing Group. Kindle Edition.

18. http://www.crosspointechurch.com/downloads/pdf_files/ pdf_baptisminfo.pdf

19. Spiros Zodhiates, *The Complete Word Study Dictionary: New Testament* (Chattanooga, TN: AMG Publishers, 2000)

20. Adrian Rogers and Steve Rogers, *What Every Christian Ought to Know* (Nashville: B&H, 2012).

ENDNOTES

21. Philip Schaff (2012-12-10). *History of The Apostolic Church* (Kindle Location 18800). Kindle Edition. (History of Apostolic Church, pp. 568-569).

22. John Calvin and Henry Beveridge, *Institutes of the Christian Religion, vol. 3* (Edinburgh: The Calvin Translation Society, 1845), 344.

23. Adrian Rogers and Steve Rogers, *What Every Christian Ought to Know* (Nashville: B&H, 2012).

24. http://www.preacherscorner.org/havner-quotes1.htm

25. *The Screwtape Letters* by C. S. Lewis

26. John F. MacArthur Jr., *Ephesians, MacArthur New Testament Commentary* (Chicago: Moody Press, 1986), 340.

27. Johnny Hunt, *Changed*, Pulpit Press.

28. Robert J. Morgan, *Nelson's Annual Preacher's Sourcebook, 2009 Edition* (Nashville, TN: Thomas Nelson Publishers), 244.

29. Achtemeier, Paul J., Harper & Row and Society of Biblical Literature. *Harper's Bible Dictionary*. San Francisco: Harper & Row, 1985.

30. David Jeremiah, *Facing the Giants in Your Life: Study Guide* (Nashville, TN: Thomas Nelson Publishers, 2001), 19.

31. Michael Bentley, *Living for Christ in a Pagan World: 1 And 2 Peter Simply Explained, Welwyn Commentary Series* (Darlington, England: Evangelical Press, 1990), 171–172.

32. Kittel, Gerhard, Gerhard Friedrich, and Geoffrey William Bromiley. *Theological Dictionary of the New Testament*. Grand Rapids, MI: W.B. Eerdmans, 1985.

33. R. Kent Hughes, *Ephesians: The Mystery of the Body of Christ, Preaching the Word* (Wheaton, IL: Crossway Books, 1990), 232.

34. *Barclay's Daily Study Bible (NT)*.

35. Warren W. Wiersbe, *The Bible Exposition Commentary, vol. 2* (Wheaton, IL: Victor Books, 1996), 58–59.

36. *The Spiritual Woman: Ten Principles of Spirituality and Women Who Have Lived*. By Lewis A. Drummond, Betty Drummond

37. https://www.barna.org/barna-update/culture/664-the-state-of-the-bible-6-trends-for-2014#.U5swhPldWSo

38. David Jeremiah, *The Power of Encouragement* (Sisters, OR: Multnomah Books, 1997), 60.

39. John Ortberg, *The Me I Want to Be* (Grand Rapids, MI: Zondervan, 2010).

40. John Ortberg, *Soul Keeping: Caring for the Most Important Part of You* (Grand Rapids, MI: Zondervan, 2014).

41. John Ortberg, *The Life You've Always Wanted: Spiritual Disciplines for Ordinary People* (Grand Rapids, MI: Zondervan, 2009).

42. *Unstuck: Your Life. God's Design. Real Change.* by Arnie Cole, Michael Ross

ENDNOTES

43. Ken Abraham, *Armed and Dangerous* (Uhrichsville, OH: Barbour, 2013).

44. Galaxie Software, *10,000 Sermon Illustrations* (Biblical Studies Press, 2002).

45. *On Second Thought: Outsmarting Your Mind's Hard-Wired Habits* by Wray Herbert

46. Robert J. Morgan, *Nelson's Complete Book of Stories, Illustrations, and Quotes, electronic ed.* (Nashville: Thomas Nelson Publishers, 2000), 66.

47. Robert J. Morgan, *Nelson's Complete Book of Stories, Illustrations, and Quotes, electronic ed.* (Nashville: Thomas Nelson Publishers, 2000), 57.

48. Ortberg, John. *The Me I Want to Be.* Grand Rapids, MI: Zondervan, 2010.

49. Richard Foster, *Celebration of Discipline*, p. 17.

50. Jim Cymbala, *Breakthrough Prayer* (Grand Rapids, MI: Zondervan, 2010).

51. http://www.beliefnet.com/Quotes/Christian/W/William- Carey/Prayer-Secret-Fervent-Believing-Prayer-Lies-At. aspx#iYClEWPJPHOSx0gt.99

52. Max Lucado, *Before Amen: The Power of a Simple Prayer* (Nashville: Thomas Nelson, 2014).

53. *Tyranny of the Urgent!* by Charles E. Hummel

54. http://www.guinnessworldrecords.com/world- records/1000/longest-time-breath-held-voluntarily-(male)

55. http://www.the7greatprayers.com/prayerstats.aspx

56. Morgan, Robert J. *Nelson's Complete Book of Stories, Illustrations, and Quotes. electronic ed.* Nashville: Thomas Nelson Publishers, 2000.

57. Thanks to Danny Lovett for this acrostic.

58. Jim Cymbala, *Breakthrough Prayer* (Grand Rapids, MI: Zondervan, 2010).

59. *The Prayer of Jabez: Breaking Through to the Blessed Life* (Breakthrough Series) by Bruce Wilkinson

60. Richard Foster, *Celebration of Discipline.*

61. Dr. Gray Allison, seminary lecture.

62. Jones, G. Curtis. *1000 Illustrations for Preaching and Teaching* (Nashville, TN: Broadman & Holman Publishers, 1986).

63. Gerhard Kittel, Gerhard Friedrich, and Geoffrey William Bromiley, *Theological Dictionary of the New Testament* (Grand Rapids, MI: W.B. Eerdmans, 1985), 186.

64. David Jeremiah, God in You: Releasing the Power of the Holy Spirit in Your Life (Sisters, OR: Multnomah Publishers, 1998), 99.

65. Spiros Zodhiates, *The Complete Word Study Dictionary: New Testament* (Chattanooga, TN: AMG Publishers, 2000).

66. William Arndt et al., *A Greek-English Lexicon of the New Testament and Other Early Christian Literature: A Translation and Adaption of the Fourth Revised*

ENDNOTES

and Augmented Edition of Walter Bauer's Griechisch-Deutsches Worterbuch Zu Den Schrift En Des Neuen Testaments Und Der Ubrigen Urchristlichen Literatur (Chicago: University of Chicago Press, 1979), 630.

67. Thayer, Joseph Henry. *A Greek-English Lexicon of the New Testament: Being Grimm's Wilke's Clavis Novi Testamenti.* New York: Harper & Brothers., 1889.

68. Frederick Dale Bruner, *Holy Spirit: Shy Member of the Trinity.* Eugene, OR: Wipf & Stock, 2001, 10.

69. Carolyn T. Ritzman, Claude King, and W. Oscar Thompson, *Concentric Circles of Concern: From Self to Others through Life- Style Evangelism* (Nashville: B&H, 1999).

70. http://www.psychologytoday.com/blog/compassion-matters/201011/generosity-what-s-in-it-you; http://www.huffingtonpost.com/2013/12/01/generosity-health_n_4323727.html; http://www.oprah.com/health/Scientific-Proof-That-Charitable-Giving-Improves-Your-Health_1; http://well.blogs.nytimes.com/2011/12/08/is-generosity-better-than-sex/?_php=true&_type=blogs&_r=0

71. http://www.allheadlinenews.com/articles/7010405366

72. Ron Blue, The New Master Your Money, p. 27.

73. http://healthland.time.com/2010/03/08/generosity-can-be-contagious/

74. http://www.thecrimson.com/article/1995/5/1/law-schools-hauser-hall-dedicated-in/

75. http://articles.latimes.com/keyword/harvard-law/recent/4

76. Dallas Willard and Jan Johnson, *Renovation of the Heart in Daily Practice: Experiments in Spiritual Transformation* (Colorado Springs, CO: NavPress, 2006), 57.

77. Larry Shallenberger, *Divine Intention: How God's Work in the Early Church Empowers Us Today* (Colorado Springs, CO: David C Cook, 2010).

78. Desire: The Journey We Must Take to Find the Life God Offers by John Eldredge

79. Quoted from John Eldredge, *The Ransomed Heart: a Collection of Devotional Readings* (Nashville: Thomas Nelson, 2005).

80. http://dictionary.reference.com/browse/imputed

www.ingramcontent.com/pod-product-compliance
Lightning Source LLC
Chambersburg PA
CBHW071729090426
42738CB00011B/2435